THIS BOOK BELONGS TO

....

DATE

....

psalms

An All-in-One Study on God's Song Book

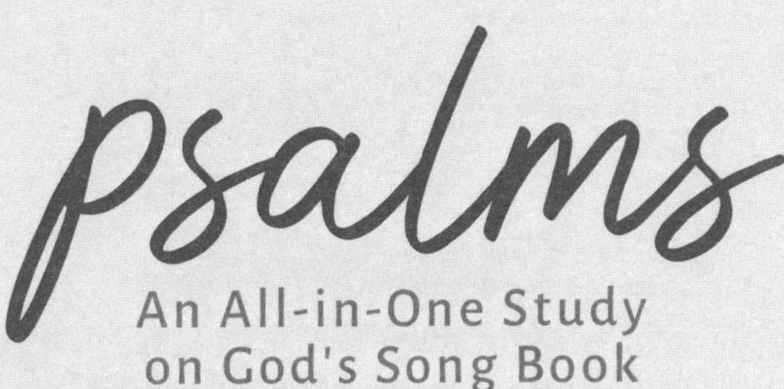
psalms
An All-in-One Study
on God's Song Book

THE
BIBLE STUDY
COLLECTIVE

BARBOUR
PUBLISHING

Editorial assistance by Tracy M. Sumner and Carey Scott.

ISBN 978-1-63609-860-9

Cover Design: Greg Jackson, Thinkpen Design

Published by Barbour Publishing, Inc., 1810 Barbour Drive, Uhrichsville, Ohio 44683, www.barbourbooks.com

Our mission is to inspire the world with the life-changing message of the Bible.

Printed in China.

Contents

THE BIBLE STUDY COLLECTIVE

Welcome to *Psalms: An All-in-One Bible Study on God's Songbook*, a collection of 30 select psalms and guidance and encouragement for digging into them yourself.

The book of Psalms has been called the "hymnbook" of the Old Testament. It is composed of 150 writings by a variety of authors. Almost half of the psalms (seventy-three) are attributed to David, with others coming from Asaph (including his descendants, one of the clans of Levites assigned to oversee the music ministry of the temple), the sons of Korah, Solomon, Moses, Heman, and Ethan. Forty-nine of the psalms have no designated author.

Each study in this guide includes an introduction of the particular psalm on the first page, followed by the full text of the psalm on the next page. The third through the fifth pages of each study highlight the three steps of what is called the "inductive method" of Bible study: observation, interpretation, and application. Here's how it works:

- ***Observation*** answers the question, "What does it say?" In other words, what is the actual content in the text?
- ***Interpretation*** answers the question, "What does it mean?" In this step, you'll consider the author's original intent and meaning.
- ***Finally***, application answers the questions, "What does it mean to you—and how can you apply it to your life?"

Each study in this guide ends with a select verse (or verses) from the psalm you've just studied, as well as related scriptures, for memorization and meditation.

Our prayer is that *Psalms: An All-in-One Bible Study on God's Songbook* will help you to better understand God's Word, and to apply its timeless truth to your own life of faith in the Lord Jesus Christ.

BARBOUR PUBLISHING

Study 1

PSALM 1

Psalm 1 serves as an introduction to the entire book of Psalms, and it sets the tone for the rest of the book. Psalm 1:1, and therefore the entire book, begins with the words, "Blessed is the man" (or woman!) showing us that this psalm addresses this all-important question: How can one be happy and blessed in this life?

Psalm 1 is called a "wisdom psalm" because it teaches the Christ follower that her own happiness comes largely as a result of a decision to faithfully follow God's direction for life. It teaches that choosing the right way leads to God's blessings, while choosing the wrong way leads to despair and misery.

Throughout scripture God calls His people to set their standards higher than those of the world. People who commit themselves to Him and are obedient to His life instructions are promised rewards; those who reject Him can expect judgment.

Psalm 1 Outline

(VERSE 1)	What a blessed/righteous person does not do
(VERSE 2)	What the righteous person does: loves and meditates on the Word of God
(VERSE 3)	The blessings of loving God and His Word
(VERSE 4)	The life of the ungodly
(VERSE 5)	The ungodly will not share in the future/eternal blessings
(VERSE 6)	The way of those who love God and His Word. . . and those who don't

1Blessed is the man who does not walk in the counsel of the ungodly or stand in the way of sinners or sit in the seat of the scornful.

2But his delight is in the law of the Lord, and on His law he meditates day and night.

3And he shall be like a tree planted by the rivers of water that brings forth its fruit in its season. His leaf also shall not wither, and whatever he does shall prosper.

4The ungodly are not so but are like the chaff that the wind drives away.

5Therefore the ungodly shall not stand in the judgment nor sinners in the congregation of the righteous.

6For the Lord knows the way of the righteous, but the way of the ungodly shall perish.

Observe

What does Psalm 1 say about the requirements for living a blessed life?

Why is it so important to avoid ungodly influences?

In what should believers delight so they may be blessed?

Interpret

What does God's Word mean by the word *blessed*?

What does Psalm 1 mean by bringing "forth its fruit in its season"?

How can you steer clear of negative influences in your own life while remaining a positive influence on others?

Apply

What is your part in "bearing fruit"?

Why is regular reading and meditation on scripture so important?

How can you make God's Word a bigger part of your daily walk with Jesus?

Psalm 1 Scripture for Memorization/Meditation

Blessed is the man who does not walk in the counsel of the ungodly or stand in the way of sinners or sit in the seat of the scornful. But his delight is in the law of the Lord, and on His law he meditates day and night.
VERSES 1–2

Verses for Further Memorization/Meditation

- Delight yourself also in the Lord, and He shall give you the desires of your heart. Commit your way to the Lord. Trust also in Him, and He shall bring it to pass (Psalm 37:4–5).
- Your word is a lamp to my feet and a light to my path (Psalm 119:105).
- "It is written, 'Man shall not live by bread alone, but by every word that proceeds out of the mouth of God' " (Matthew 4:4).
- All scripture is given by inspiration of God and is profitable for doctrine, for reproof, for correction, for instruction in righteousness, that the man of God may be perfect, thoroughly furnished for all good works (2 Timothy 3:16–17).
- For the word of God is living and powerful and sharper than any two-edged sword, piercing even to the dividing of soul and spirit, and of the joints and marrow, and is a discerner of the thoughts and intentions of the heart (Hebrews 4:12).

Study 2

PSALM 6

David's whole body is afflicted with pain. David is sick of being sick—worn out from groaning and weeping. With his bones in agony and soul in anguish, his whole being is in pain and he knows that only God can heal him, only God can have mercy on him. He asks God, "How long?" and begs the Lord to bring an end to the chastening he knows is a big part of his suffering.

David expresses his hopeful heart for healing because he believes in God's unfailing love. He cries out to God, saying that he can continue to acknowledge God as long as he is living, but death will put an end to his ability to praise Him.

Psalm 6 Outline

(VERSE 1)	David's plea for relief from God's chastening hand
(VERSES 2–3)	David's troubles
(VERSES 4–5)	David's urgent plea
(VERSES 6–7)	A detailed, vivid description of David's misery
(VERSES 8–10)	David's confidence in God's listening ear

To the chief musician on neginoth on sheminith, a psalm of David.

1 O Lord, do not rebuke me in Your anger or chasten me in Your hot displeasure.

2 Have mercy on me, O Lord, for I am weak. O Lord, heal me, for my bones are vexed.

3 My soul is also greatly vexed, but You, O Lord, how long?

4 Return, O Lord, deliver my soul. Oh save me for Your mercies' sake.

5 For in death there is no remembrance of You. In the grave who shall give You thanks?

6 I am weary with my groaning; all night I make my bed to swim. I water my couch with my tears.

7 My eye is consumed because of grief. It grows old because of all my enemies.

8 Depart from me, all you workers of iniquity, for the Lord has heard the sound of my weeping.

9 The Lord has heard my supplication; the Lord will receive my prayer.

10 Let all my enemies be ashamed and greatly vexed. Let them return and be ashamed suddenly.

Observe

What key words in this psalm describe David's mental and emotional state when he wrote it?

What requests does David make of God?

How does the way this psalm ends demonstrate David's hope and confidence in God?

Interpret

What does Psalm 6 say about how we should respond to weariness and sickness in our own lives?

How should a woman of God approach Him when she feels under God's hand of discipline?

Why does God chasten or discipline His people?

Apply

What is the best way to respond when you know you are under God's hand of discipline?

....

....

....

....

....

....

What should you do when you are suffering, and you want to know why?

....

....

....

....

....

....

How can you know God hears you when it doesn't *feel* like He's listening?

....

....

....

....

....

Psalm 6 Scriptures for Memorization/Meditation

Return, O Lord, deliver my soul.
Oh save me for Your mercies' sake.
VERSE 4

The Lord has heard my supplication; the
Lord will receive my prayer.
VERSE 9

Related Verses for Further Memorization/Meditation

- "You shall also consider in your heart that as a man chastens his son, so the Lord your God chastens you" (Deuteronomy 8:5).
- My son, do not despise the discipline of the Lord or be weary of His correction. For those whom the Lord loves, He corrects, like a father with the son in whom he delights (Proverbs 3:11–12).
- If you endure chastening, God deals with you as with sons, for what son is he whom the father does not chasten? But if you are without chastisement, of which all are partakers, then you are illegitimate children and not sons (Hebrews 12:7–8).
- "As many as I love, I rebuke and chasten. Therefore be zealous and repent" (Revelation 3:19).

Study 3
PSALM 9

Like several of the preceding psalms of David, Psalm 9 deals with his struggles to endure the persecution of his enemies. David is eager to sing and rejoice because God has dealt with his foes. They have been not only defeated but also rebuked, destroyed, and blotted out. Their ruin is sure, and soon there will not even be a memory of them.

David begins to extol the character of God. He affirms that the Lord is an eternal king, a righteous judge, and a stronghold and refuge for those needing help. People who seek God, he says, can count on Him to come through for them.

As for the nations, they will reap what they have sown. What they plotted against others will be their own downfall. Those who humbly seek the Lord, on the other hand, will receive His blessings and see Him bring glory to Himself.

Psalm 9 Outline

(VERSES 1–2) David's song of praise for the God who does great things

(VERSES 3–5) David's praise for the God who defends him against his enemies

(VERSES 6–8) A celebration of God's victory

(VERSES 9–10) Declarations of trust in God as a refuge

(VERSES 11–12) God remembers His people

(VERSES 13–14) David's plea for God's mercy

(VERSES 15–16) The ultimate destiny of the ungodly

(VERSES 17–18) How God deals with the wicked. . .and the humble

(VERSES 19–20) God will glorify Himself

To the chief musician on Muth-labben, a psalm of David.

1 I will praise You, O LORD, with my whole heart; I will show forth
all Your marvelous works.
2 I will be glad and rejoice in You. I will sing praise to Your
name, O You Most High.
3 When my enemies turn back, they shall fall and perish in
Your presence.
4 For You have maintained my right and my cause; You sat on
the throne judging righteously.
5 You have rebuked the nations. You have destroyed the wicked.
You have put out their name forever and ever.
6 O you enemy, destructions have come to a perpetual end, and
you have destroyed cities. Their memorial has perished with them.
7 But the LORD shall endure forever. He has prepared His
throne for judgment.
8 And He shall judge the world in righteousness. He shall
minister judgment to the people in uprightness.
9 The LORD also will be a refuge for the oppressed, a refuge
in times of trouble.
10 And those who know Your name will put their trust in You,
for You, LORD, have not forsaken those who seek You.
11 Sing praises to the LORD, who dwells in Zion. Declare among
the people His doings.
12 When He avenges blood, He remembers them. He does not
forget the cry of the humble.
13 Have mercy on me, O LORD. Consider my trouble that I
suffer from those who hate me, You who lifts me up from the
gates of death,
14 That I may show forth all Your praise in the gates of the
daughter of Zion. I will rejoice in Your salvation.
15 The nations have sunk down in the pit that they made; their
own foot has been caught in the net that they hid.
16 The LORD is known by the judgment that He executes.
The wicked person is ensnared by the work of his own hands.
Higgaion. Selah.
17 The wicked shall return to hell, and all the nations who
forget God.

[18]For the needy shall not always be forgotten. The expectation
of the poor shall not perish forever.
[19]Arise, O LORD. Let man not prevail. Let the nations be judged
in Your sight.
[20]Put them in fear, O LORD, that the nations may know themselves to be but men. *Selah*.

Observe

What theme or themes run throughout this psalm?

What does it teach about God's character?

Why did David call people to praise the Lord?

Interpret

As believers, how do our words and actions influence how others might perceive God?

What does this psalm call us to do?

How does God want us to handle our fears, worries, and anxious thoughts?

Apply

What is the best way to pray when you are concerned about a wicked or unjust practice?

....

....

....

....

....

How can you wisely follow David's example in this psalm?

....

....

....

....

....

....

How can you show gratitude to the Lord for the ways He helped and delivered you in times of trouble?

....

....

....

....

....

....

....

Psalm 9 Scriptures for Memorization/Meditation

I will praise You, O LORD, with my whole heart;
I will show forth all Your marvelous works.
VERSE 1

Sing praises to the LORD, who dwells in Zion.
Declare among the people His doings.
VERSE 11

Verses for Further Memorization/Meditation

- "For the LORD your God is He who goes with you, to fight for you against your enemies, to save you" (Deuteronomy 20:4).
- ". . .because He has appointed a day on which He will judge the world in righteousness by that Man whom He has ordained, in which He has given assurance to all men in that He has raised Him from the dead" (Acts 17:31).
- No, in all these things we are more than conquerors through Him who loved us (Romans 8:37).
- Therefore let us come boldly to the throne of grace, that we may obtain mercy and find grace to help in time of need (Hebrews 4:16).

Study 4

PSALM 16

Psalm 16's superscription includes the first mention of a *michtam*, another presumed but undeterminable musical term. The word appears in later psalms (56–60), where David describes himself in personal peril. In this case, David may be in fear of a threat of some sort, although throughout most of the psalm, he expresses overwhelming confidence and optimism because He feels certain God is his refuge, which he affirms in other psalms (2:12; 7:1; 9:9).

God is David's solitary source of comfort and safety. His expression of faithful confidence in the Lord in verses 7–10 is so powerful that this psalm is later quoted by both Peter (Acts 2:25–28) and Paul (Acts 13:35). After the life, death, and resurrection of Jesus, David's words about death take on a surprising new significance.

Psalm 16 Outline

(VERSES 1–3)	David's declaration of confidence in his God
(VERSES 4–6)	The sorrow of idolatry and the blessing of honoring the one true God
(VERSES 7–8)	The benefits of God's guidance and counsel
(VERSES 9–11)	The joy in knowing and following the Lord

Michtam of David.

1 Preserve me, O God, for in You I put my trust.
2 O my soul, you have said to the LORD, "You are my Lord; my
goodness does not extend to You,
3 but to the saints who are in the earth, and to the excellent,
in whom is all my delight."
4 The sorrows of those who hurry after another god shall be
multiplied. I will not offer their drink offerings of blood or take
up their names on my lips.
5 The LORD is the portion of my inheritance and of my cup.
You maintain my lot.
6 The lines have fallen to me in pleasant places. Yes, I have a
beautiful heritage.
7 I will bless the LORD, who has given me counsel. My mind
also instructs me in the night seasons.
8 I have set the LORD always before me; because He is at my
right hand, I shall not be moved.
9 Therefore my heart is glad, and my glory rejoices. My flesh
also shall rest in hope.
10 For You will not leave my soul in hell, nor will You allow Your
Holy One to see corruption.
11 You will show me the path of life. In Your presence is fullness of joy; at Your right hand there are pleasures forevermore.

Observe

What does Psalm 16 say about God's attitude toward believers?

In verse 2, what do we see about David's attitude toward the Lord?

What does this psalm say about following "another god"?

Interpret

What good things do believers receive from the Lord?

How does a woman of God "set the Lord always before" her?

How does God view unbelievers?

Apply

In what ways does God "counsel" you?

....

....

....

....

....

What does it mean that "My mind also instructs me in the night seasons"?

....

....

....

....

....

....

How does it affect your thoughts and attitude to realize that everything good you have is from God?

....

....

....

....

....

....

Psalm 16 Scripture for Memorization/Meditation

You will show me the path of life. In Your presence is fullness of joy; at Your right hand there are pleasures forevermore.
VERSE 11

Verses for Further Memorization/Meditation

- The idols of the nations are silver and gold, the work of men's hands. They have mouths, but they do not speak; they have eyes, but they do not see; they have ears, but they do not hear; nor is there any breath in their mouths. Those who make them are like them; so is everyone who trusts in them (Psalm 135:15–18).
- Therefore I beseech you, brothers, by the mercies of God, that you present your bodies as a living sacrifice, holy, acceptable to God, which is your reasonable service. And do not be conformed to this world, but be transformed by the renewing of your mind, that you may prove what is that good and acceptable and perfect will of God (Romans 12:1–2).
- Let your conduct be without covetousness, and be content with what you have, for He has said, "I will never leave you or forsake you." So we may boldly say, "The Lord is my helper, and I will not fear what man shall do to me" (Hebrews 13:5–6).
- Little children, keep yourselves from idols. Amen (1 John 5:21).

Study 5
PSALM 19

David begins Psalm 19 by giving attention to the natural world that reflects God's glory and then moves on to the revealed Word of God—the source of many blessings. After looking into the heavens to witness the glory of God, David looks to the Word of God: its laws, statutes, promises, commands, and ordinances. To him, an awareness of God's Word results both in practical help (wisdom, righteousness, and warning) and in positive, pleasant feelings (joy, enlightenment).

David's personal knowledge of God inspires him toward devotion to his Lord. He wants to rid his life of willful sins as well as hidden faults. David ends this psalm with a prayer that not only his words but also his inner thoughts would be pleasing to God, his strength and redeemer.

Psalm 19 Outline

(VERSES 1–2)	God reveals Himself and demonstrates His glory through His creation
(VERSES 3–6)	God speaks through His creation
(VERSES 7–8)	God reveals Himself and His desires for us through His Word
(VERSES 9–12)	Our proper response to God's revelation—fear
(VERSES 13–14)	Asking God for His help in thinking, speaking, and living in ways that please Him

To the chief musician, a psalm of David.

1 The heavens declare the glory of God, and the heavens proclaim His handiwork.

2 Day to day utters speech, and night to night reveals knowledge.

3 There is no speech or language where their voice is not heard.

4 Their line has gone out through all the earth, and their words to the end of the world. In them He has set a tabernacle for the sun,

5 which is like a bridegroom coming out of his chamber, and rejoices as a strong man to run a race.

6 Its going forth is from the end of the heaven, and its circuit to the ends of it, and there is nothing hidden from its heat.

7 The law of the Lord is perfect, converting the soul. The testimony of the Lord is sure, making wise the simple.

8 The statutes of the Lord are right, rejoicing the heart. The commandment of the Lord is pure, enlightening the eyes.

9 The fear of the Lord is clean, enduring forever. The judgments of the Lord are true and righteous altogether.

10 More to be desired are they than gold, yes, than very fine gold; sweeter also than honey and the honeycomb.

11 Moreover Your servant is warned by them, and in keeping them there is great reward.

12 Who can understand his errors? You cleanse me from secret faults.

13 Keep back Your servant also from presumptuous sins; let them not have dominion over me. Then I shall be upright, and I shall be innocent of the great transgression.

14 Let the words of my mouth and the meditation of my heart be acceptable in Your sight, O Lord, my strength and my redeemer.

Observe

What does creation have to say to us about God Himself?

What did David say in Psalm 19 about God's law (or Word)?

What desire did David state in verses 13–14?

Interpret

What role should God's Word play in the everyday life of the believer?

How does God approach our sins, faults, and imperfections?

As godly women, how should we approach the Word of God?

Apply

How can you develop a deep appreciation and hunger for God's written Word?

How can you best protect yourself from a life of sin and rebellion?

What changes do you need to make so that your thoughts and words please the Lord?

Psalm 19 Scriptures for Memorization/Meditation

The law of the Lord is perfect, converting the soul. The testimony of the Lord is sure, making wise the simple. The statutes of the Lord are right, rejoicing the heart. The commandment of the Lord is pure, enlightening the eyes.
VERSES 7–8

Let the words of my mouth and the meditation
of my heart be acceptable in Your sight,
O Lord, my strength and my redeemer.
VERSE 14

Verses for Further Memorization/Meditation

- And God said, "Let Us make man in Our image, according to Our likeness, and let them have dominion over the fish of the sea, and over the fowl of the air, and over the cattle, and over all the earth, and over every creeping thing that creeps on the earth" (Genesis 1:26).
- O Lord, You open my lips, and my mouth shall declare Your praise (Psalm 51:15).
- In the beginning was the Word, and the Word was with God, and the Word was God. The same was in the beginning with God. All things were made by Him, and without Him nothing was made that was made (John 1:1–3).
- . . .who, being the brightness of His glory and the express image of His person, and upholding all things by the word of His power, when He had by Himself purged our sins, sat down at the right hand of the Majesty on high (Hebrews 1:3).
- If we confess our sins, He is faithful and just to forgive us our sins and to cleanse us from all unrighteousness (1 John 1:9).

Study 6

PSALM 20

Psalm 20 was written for an assembled group to join the king in prayer preceding a battle. Significant spiritual preparation has already taken place. The king's prayers have been offered to God, along with sacrifices at the tabernacle (sanctuary). Battle plans have been made and David is mentally ready, but he wants to ensure that God is with him and that he has the support of the people. And indeed, the people are anticipating a joyous victory.

The singular voice may be that of David, the king. Or possibly it is a response assigned to a designated Levite participating in the worship ceremony. Even though the crowd is expecting victory, the credit goes to God before the battle even begins.

Psalm 20 Outline

(VERSES 1–2)	The Lord's answer and help in times of trouble
(VERSE 3)	The Lord receives our sacrifices and offerings
(VERSE 4)	God fulfills our desires and purposes
(VERSE 5)	The Lord answers our prayers
(VERSE 6)	God saves all who are His
(VERSE 7)	We can trust in the name of the Lord
(VERSES 8–9)	The power in trusting in the Lord

To the chief musician, a psalm of David.

1 May the Lord hear you in the day of trouble. May the name of
the God of Jacob defend you.
2 May He send you help from the sanctuary and strengthen
you out of Zion.
3 May He remember all your offerings and accept your burnt
sacrifice. *Selah.*
4 May He grant you according to your own heart and fulfill
all your purpose.
5 We will rejoice in your salvation, and in the name of our God
we will set up our banners. May the Lord fulfill all your petitions.
6 Now I know that the Lord saves His anointed. He will hear him
from His holy heaven with the saving strength of His right hand.
7 Some trust in chariots and some in horses, but we will
remember the name of the Lord our God.
8 They have been brought down and fallen, but we have risen
and stand upright.
9 Save, Lord. Let the King hear us when we call.

Observe

What is prayed for in this psalm?

What wonderful promises are listed?

What approach to God is presented in Psalm 20?

Interpret

What is suggested about the importance of faith?

What does this psalm say about the importance of prayer?

What benefits of trusting the Lord are listed?

Apply

In what ways can Psalm 20 encourage and instruct you in your prayer life during times of trouble?

Why is it dangerous to put your trust in anything or anyone other than the Lord?

How is your heart encouraged by the truths in this psalm?

Psalm 20 Scripture for Memorization/Meditation

Some trust in chariots and some in horses, but we will remember the name of the LORD our God.
VERSE 7

Verses for Further Memorization/Meditation

- Trust in Him at all times. You people, pour out your heart before Him. God is a refuge for us. *Selah* (Psalm 62:8).
- The LORD is good, a stronghold in the day of trouble, and He knows those who trust in Him (Nahum 1:7).
- "Therefore I say to you, whatever things you desire when you pray, believe that you have received them, and you shall have them" (Mark 11:24).
- "For the eyes of the Lord are on the righteous, and His ears are open to their prayers, but the face of the Lord is against those who do evil" (1 Peter 3:12).

Study 7

PSALM 23

In one of the best known and most beloved of the psalms, David uses the imagery of a shepherd and his sheep to underscore God's blessings, provision, and protection of His people. In biblical times, kings were commonly likened to shepherds. In Psalm 23, however, David was one of the sheep in the fold of God.

David described the Lord as a good shepherd—a title Jesus applied to Himself centuries later (John 10:11). As the greatest shepherd, God provides for every need of His sheep. The green pastures and quiet waters are basic physical needs, but God also restores the soul, attending to the inner spiritual needs of humankind. Guidance is another role of ancient shepherds. In a land where many of the paths are rocky and treacherous, the safety of the sheep reflects on the reputation of the shepherd.

Study Outline

(VERSE 1)	A declaration of God's relationship with David
(VERSE 2)	God, the Shepherd who sustains
(VERSE 3)	The Shepherd who restores and leads
(VERSE 4)	The Shepherd's comforting presence
(VERSE 5)	Blessings in times of danger
(VERSE 6)	Assurance of future blessings

A psalm of David.

1 The LORD is my shepherd. I shall not want.
2 He makes me to lie down in green pastures. He leads me
beside the still waters.
3 He restores my soul. He leads me in the paths of righteousness for His name's sake.
4 Yes, though I walk through the valley of the shadow of death,
I will not fear evil, for You are with me. Your rod and Your staff,
they comfort me.
5 You prepare a table before me in the presence of my enemies.
You anoint my head with oil. My cup runs over.
6 Surely goodness and mercy shall follow me all the days of
my life, and I will dwell in the house of the LORD forever.

Observe

What benefits did David enjoy as one of God's beloved "sheep"?

How did David's relationship with his Shepherd-God affect his response to fear and danger?

How did David see his future?

PSALM 23

Interpret

How did seeing God as his loving Shepherd shape David's relationship with the Lord?

....

....

....

....

....

What did David mean when he wrote "My cup runs over"?

....

....

....

....

....

....

What thoughts and emotions did David express most strongly in Psalm 23?

....

....

....

....

....

....

....

Apply

In what ways have you seen God demonstrate His goodness and provision to you personally?

....

....

....

....

....

How should you respond when you're feeling overwhelmed by fear or grief?

....

....

....

....

....

....

How do you view your future—in this life and in the life to come?

....

....

....

....

....

....

Psalm 23 Scripture for Memorization/Meditation

Surely goodness and mercy shall follow me all the days of my life, and I will dwell in the house of the Lord forever.
VERSE 6

Verses for Further Memorization/Meditation

- Like a shepherd, He shall feed His flock. He shall gather the lambs with His arm and carry them in His bosom, and shall gently lead those who are with young (Isaiah 40:11).
- "I am the good shepherd. The good shepherd gives His life for the sheep" (John 10:11).
- Now may the God of peace, who brought again from the dead our Lord Jesus, that great Shepherd of the sheep, through the blood of the everlasting covenant, make you perfect in every good work to do His will, working in you what is well pleasing in His sight, through Jesus Christ, to whom be glory forever and ever. Amen (Hebrews 13:20–21).
- For you were as sheep going astray but are now returned to the Shepherd and Bishop of your souls (1 Peter 2:25).

Study 8

PSALM 27

In his psalms, including this one, David wrote of the universal emotion of fear. When afraid, some people muster all the courage they can and stand their ground. At the first sign of trouble, others flee so that they can live to fight another day.

David begins this psalm with his own questions about fear and concludes it with another option for responding to fear that involves neither standing and fighting nor turning and fleeing. He has obviously given the matter of fear much more thought than most of us, because he has already determined that God is his light, salvation, and defense. He will not stumble in the darkness, as many do. He has a deliverer and security, even during the times that are most alarming. David prays that God will continue to be merciful and available, and he believes that God will be there during the worst of times, when even those closest to him might walk away.

Psalm 27 Outline

(VERSES 1–3)	David's confidence in his God
(VERSE 4)	David desires God's presence
(VERSES 5–6)	The blessings of God's presence
(VERSES 7–10)	Seeking hard after the faithful God
(VERSES 11–13)	A prayer for God's guidance
(VERSE 14)	Encouragement to wait on the Lord

A psalm of David.

[1]The LORD is my light and my salvation. Whom shall I fear? The LORD is the strength of my life. Of whom shall I be afraid?

[2]When the wicked, even my enemies and my foes, came on me to eat up my flesh, they stumbled and fell.

[3]Though an army should encamp against me, my heart shall not fear. Though war should rise against me, in this I will be confident.

[4]One thing I have asked of the LORD, that I will seek after: that I may dwell in the house of the LORD all the days of my life, to behold the beauty of the LORD and to inquire in His temple.

[5]For in the time of trouble He shall hide me in His pavilion, in the secret of His tabernacle He shall hide me. He shall set me up on a rock.

[6]And now my head shall be lifted up above my enemies around me. Therefore I will offer in His tabernacle sacrifices of joy. I will sing, yes, I will sing praises to the LORD.

[7]Hear, O LORD, when I cry with my voice. Have mercy also on me and answer me.

[8]When You said, "Seek My face," my heart said to You, "Your face, LORD, I will seek."

[9]Do not hide Your face far from me. Do not put Your servant away in anger. You have been my help. Do not leave me or forsake me, O God of my salvation.

[10]When my father and my mother forsake me, then the LORD will take me up.

[11]Teach me Your way, O LORD, and lead me in a plain path, because of my enemies.

[12]Do not deliver me over to the will of my enemies, for false witnesses have risen up against me and those who breathe out cruelty.

[13]I would have lost strength, but I believed I would see the goodness of the LORD in the land of the living.

[14]Wait on the LORD. Be of good courage, and He shall strengthen your heart. Wait, I say, on the LORD.

Observe

How and why could David so confidently face his fears?

What dangers was David facing when he wrote this psalm?

What was the basis for David's confident hope that the Lord would hear his prayer and have mercy on him?

Interpret

What kept David from losing heart even though he faced opposition?

What is the key to being of good courage?

What did David passionately desire of his God?

Apply

How can you follow David's example when you feel worried or afraid?

How can you faithfully respond as a believer when someone speaks lies about you?

What are some practical ways you deepen your relationship with God?

Psalm 27 Scriptures for Memorization/Meditation

The Lord is my light and my salvation. Whom shall I fear? The Lord is the strength of my life. Of whom shall I be afraid?
VERSE 1

One thing I have asked of the Lord, that I will seek after: that I may dwell in the house of the Lord all the days of my life, to behold the beauty of the Lord and to inquire in His temple.
VERSE 4

Verses for Further Memorization/Meditation

- Trust in the Lord with all your heart and do not lean on your own understanding. In all your ways acknowledge Him, and He shall direct your paths (Proverbs 3:5–6).
- Even the youths shall faint and be weary, and the young men shall utterly fall, but those who wait on the Lord shall renew their strength. They shall mount up with wings like eagles, they shall run and not be weary, and they shall walk and not faint (Isaiah 40:30–31).
- For God has not given us the spirit of fear, but of power and of love and of a sound mind (2 Timothy 1:7).
- Draw near to God and He will draw near to you (James 4:8).

Study 9
PSALM 30

In Psalm 30, David writes of being in the depths, of enemies eager to gloat over his vulnerable position—perhaps even of a near-death experience. Yet he joyfully states that God has responded to his difficulties with deliverance, healing, and life.

David's confession is true for many people. When life is going well and we are feeling secure, we lose the pressing need to turn to God. Then we become dismayed that we have lost touch with Him. Yet God's mercy is abundant. David's wailing in sackcloth quickly turns to dancing for joy. He senses that God prefers songs and praise to the silence that accompanies mourning. And in response to the fresh start that God has allowed him, David will be forever thankful.

Psalm 30 Outline

(VERSE 1)	David thanks the Lord for victory over his enemies
(VERSE 2)	David thanks God for healing
(VERSE 3)	David thanks God for preserving his life
(VERSES 4–5)	An encouragement to praise the Lord
(VERSES 6–7)	David's testimony of troubled times
(VERSES 8–10)	A prayer from a time of trouble
(VERSES 11–12)	Rejoicing in answered prayer

A psalm and song at the dedication of the house of David.

1 I will extol You, O LORD, for You have lifted me up and have not
made my foes to rejoice over me.

2 O LORD my God, I cried to You, and You have healed me.

3 O LORD, You have brought up my soul from the grave. You
have kept me alive, that I should not go down to the pit.

4 Sing to the LORD, O you saints of His, and give thanks at the
remembrance of His holiness.

5 For His anger endures but a moment; in His favor is life.
Weeping may endure for a night, but joy comes in the morning.

6 And in my prosperity I said, "I shall never be moved."

7 LORD, by Your favor You have made my mountain to stand
strong. You hid Your face, and I was troubled.

8 I cried to You, O LORD, and to the LORD I made supplication:

9 "What profit is there in my blood when I go down to the pit?
Shall the dust praise You? Shall it declare Your truth?

10 Hear, O LORD, and have mercy on me. LORD, be my helper."

11 You have turned for me my mourning into dancing. You have
put off my sackcloth and girded me with gladness,

12 to the end that my glory may sing praise to You and not be
silent. O LORD my God, I will give thanks to You forever.

Observe

What is the main theme of Psalm 30?

For what does David thank and praise God?

What did David do when he felt distance between himself and God?

Interpret

What does this psalm say about divine healing?

In what ways is praising God so important in this psalm?

What does the writer say about reaching out to God when we feel that our relationship with Him is "out of sorts"?

What can you do when you feel like God is hiding His face from you?

Do you regularly thank God for healing and restoring you?

In what circumstances have you seen God turn your "mourning into dancing"?

PSALM 30

Psalm 30 Scriptures for Memorization/Meditation

Sing to the Lord, O you saints of His, and give thanks at the remembrance of His holiness.
VERSE 4

You have turned for me my mourning into dancing. You have put off my sackcloth and girded me with gladness.
VERSE 11

Verses for Further Memorization/Meditation

- "I have spoken these things to you, that in Me you might have peace. In the world you shall have tribulation, but be of good cheer: I have overcome the world" (John 16:33).
- Be anxious for nothing, but in everything, by prayer and supplication with thanksgiving, let your requests be made known to God. And the peace of God, which passes all understanding, shall guard your hearts and minds through Christ Jesus (Philippians 4:6–7).
- Let everything that has breath praise the Lord. Praise the Lord (Psalm 150:6).
- "And it shall come to pass, that before they call, I will answer, and while they are still speaking, I will hear" (Isaiah 65:24).

Study 10

PSALM 34

David's introduction to Psalm 34 explains that it is written with a specific incident in mind. When David was running from King Saul and hiding out in Philistine territory, he began to feel threatened. As a diversion, he pretended to be insane, doodling on the city gate and drooling. The Philistines insisted that he leave, but he apparently posed no threat, so his life was not threatened (1 Samuel 21:10–15).

David affirms that the angel of the Lord will encircle and deliver those who trust God. In several stories of the Old Testament, the angel of the Lord turns out to be God Himself, but any of the Lord's messengers are equipped to protect His people.

Perhaps some people are on the verge of becoming more devoted to God. For them to go on about their lives without making that decision is like walking past an enormous feast without stopping to sample the food. David urges his readers to "taste and see that the LORD is good."

Psalm 34 Outline

(VERSES 1–2) A life filled with praise

(VERSES 3–7) David's testimony of deliverance

(VERSES 8–10) The goodness of God

(VERSES 11–14) The fear of the Lord

(VERSES 15–16) The watchful eye of God

(VERSES 17–18) God helps the humble

(VERSES 19–22) God's care for His people

A psalm of David, when he changed his behavior before Abimelech, who drove him away, and he departed.

1 I will bless the LORD at all times. His praise shall continually be
in my mouth.
2 My soul shall make its boast in the LORD. The humble shall
hear of it and be glad.
3 O magnify the LORD with me, and let us exalt His name together.
4 I sought the LORD, and He heard me and delivered me from
all my fears.
5 They looked to Him and were radiant, and their faces were
not ashamed.
6 This poor man cried, and the LORD heard him and saved him
out of all his troubles.
7 The angel of the LORD encamps around those who fear him
and delivers them.
8 O taste and see that the LORD is good. Blessed is the man
who trusts in Him.
9 O fear the LORD, you His saints, for there is nothing lacking
for those who fear Him.
10 The young lions lack and suffer hunger, but those who seek
the LORD shall not lack any good thing.
11 Come, you children, listen to me. I will teach you the fear
of the LORD.
12 What man is he who desires life and loves many days, that
he may see good?
13 Keep your tongue from evil and your lips from speaking deceit.
14 Depart from evil and do good. Seek peace, and pursue it.
15 The eyes of the LORD are on the righteous, and His ears are
open to their cry.
16 The face of the LORD is against those who do evil, to cut off
the remembrance of them from the earth.
17 The righteous cry, and the LORD hears and delivers them
out of all their troubles.
18 The LORD is near to those who are of a broken heart and
saves those who have a contrite spirit.
19 Many are the afflictions of the righteous, but the LORD

delivers him out of them all.

[20]He keeps all his bones. Not one of them is broken.

[21]Evil shall slay the wicked, and those who hate the righteous shall be desolate.

[22]The LORD redeems the soul of His servants, and none of those who trust in Him shall be desolate.

Observe

What did David *choose* to do in verse 1?

....

....

....

....

For what did David praise the Lord in this psalm?

....

....

....

....

What does David say about fearing God?

....

....

....

....

....

Interpret

In what ways is praising God a choice?

What does it mean to bless the Lord "at all times"?

What does it mean to "boast in the LORD"?

Apply

What are the benefits of being counted as "righteous"?

....

....

....

....

....

....

How do you respond when faced with suffering or trouble?

....

....

....

....

....

....

How does God meet you in those moments when your heart is broken, and you have humbled yourself before Him?

....

....

....

....

....

....

....

Psalm 34 Scriptures for Memorization/Meditation

I sought the Lord, and He heard me and
delivered me from all my fears.
VERSE 4

The eyes of the Lord are on the righteous,
and His ears are open to their cry.
VERSE 15

Verses for Further Memorization/Meditation

- Therefore by Him let us continually offer the sacrifice of praise to God—that is, the fruit of our lips giving thanks to His name (Hebrews 13:15).
- . . .giving thanks to the Father, who has made us suitable to be partakers of the inheritance of the saints in light, who has delivered us from the power of darkness and has translated us to the kingdom of His dear Son (Colossians 1:12–13).
- The fear of the Lord is the beginning of knowledge, but fools despise wisdom and instruction (Proverbs 1:7).
- Therefore there is now no condemnation for those who are in Christ Jesus, who walk according to the Spirit, not according to the flesh. For the law of the Spirit of life in Christ Jesus has made me free from the law of sin and death (Romans 8:1–2).

Study 11

PSALM 37

In Psalm 37, David makes a crucial observation about wicked people that will make a critical difference in how people view them. Whatever seems to be in their favor now won't be true for long because they will soon wither like grass.

David points out that those who trust in the Lord have the opportunity and privilege of lasting rewards for their actions. And in the meantime, their relationship with God assures them of rewards that have real value. They have a good place to live, in secure surroundings. They have the desires of their hearts because the source of their delight is God.

The wicked, David holds, get away with lies, cheating, and deceit. When witnessing such injustice, God's people have one of two choices: they can worry and respond with great anger (a natural response), but that will only lead to more evil; or they can realize that God is aware of the problem and wait for Him to act. Only then will true justice be ensured.

Psalm 37 Outline

(VERSES 1–2) Do not envy evildoers

(VERSES 3–8) Trust God and delight in Him

(VERSES 9–17) The futility of an ungodly life

(VERSES 18–26) The blessings of righteousness

(VERSES 27–33) Blessings for those who obey the Lord

(VERSES 34–36) Destruction for the wicked

(VERSES 37–40) Reward for the blameless and the upright

A psalm of David.

1 Do not fret because of evildoers or be envious of the workers of iniquity.

2 For they shall soon be cut down like the grass and wither as the green herb.

3 Trust in the Lord, and do good, so you shall dwell in the land and truly you shall be fed.

4 Delight yourself also in the Lord, and He shall give you the desires of your heart.

5 Commit your way to the Lord. Trust also in Him, and He shall bring it to pass.

6 And He shall bring forth your righteousness as the light and your judgment as the noonday.

7 Rest in the Lord, and wait patiently for Him. Do not fret because of him who prospers in his way, because of the man who brings wicked schemes to pass.

8 Cease from anger, and forsake wrath. Do not fret in this way to do evil.

9 For evildoers shall be cut off, but those who wait on the Lord, they shall inherit the earth.

10 For yet a little while, and the wicked shall not be. Yes, you shall diligently consider his place, and it shall not be.

11 But the meek shall inherit the earth and shall delight themselves in the abundance of peace.

12 The wicked plots against the just and gnashes at him with his teeth.

13 The Lord shall laugh at him, for He sees that his day is coming.

14 The wicked have drawn out the sword and have bent their bow to cast down the poor and needy and to slay those who are of upright behavior.

15 Their sword shall enter into their own heart, and their bows shall be broken.

16 A little that a righteous man has is better than the riches of many wicked.

17 For the arms of the wicked shall be broken, but the Lord upholds the righteous.

18 The LORD knows the days of the upright, and their inheritance shall be forever.
19 They shall not be ashamed in the evil time, and in the days
of famine they shall be satisfied.
20 But the wicked shall perish, and the enemies of the LORD
shall be as the fat of lambs. They shall vanish; into smoke they
shall vanish away.
21 The wicked borrows and does not repay, but the righteous
shows mercy and gives.
22 For those who are blessed by Him shall inherit the earth,
and those who are cursed by Him shall be cut off.
23 The steps of a good man are ordered by the LORD, and He
delights in his way.
24 Though he falls, he shall not be utterly cast down, for the
LORD upholds him with His hand.
25 I have been young, and now am old, yet I have not seen the
righteous forsaken or his descendants begging for bread.
26 He is ever merciful and lends, and his descendants are blessed.
27 Depart from evil and do good, and dwell forevermore.
28 For the LORD loves justice and does not forsake His saints;
they are preserved forever, but the descendants of the wicked
shall be cut off.
29 The righteous shall inherit the land and dwell in it forever.
30 The mouth of the righteous speaks wisdom, and his tongue
speaks of justice.
31 The law of his God is in his heart; none of his steps shall slide.
32 The wicked watches the righteous and seeks to slay him.
33 The LORD will not leave him in his hand or condemn him
when he is judged.
34 Wait on the LORD and keep His way, and He shall exalt you
to inherit the land. When the wicked are cut off, you shall see it.
35 I have seen the wicked in great power and spreading himself
like a green bay tree.
36 Yet he passed away, and behold, he was no more. Yes,
I sought him, but he could not be found.
37 Observe the perfect man and look at the upright,
for the end of that man is peace.

[38]But the transgressors shall be destroyed together; the end
of the wicked shall be cut off.
[39]But the salvation of the righteous is of the LORD; He is their
strength in the time of trouble.
[40]And the LORD shall help them and deliver them; He shall
deliver them from the wicked and save them, because they
trust in Him.

Observe

What advice does this psalm offer concerning how to respond to evil people?

....

....

....

Why should righteous people not envy the wicked?

....

....

....

....

What are the powerful results of fully trusting in the Lord?

....

....

....

....

....

Interpret

What does this psalm say believers should do instead of worrying about the success of evildoers?

....

....

How does God show His delight in people?

....

....

What blessings do the righteous enjoy?

....

....

Apply

What does this passage teach us about envy?

....

....

As a woman of God, how can you guard your heart against envy or greed?

....

....

What blessings from the Lord do you enjoy?

....

....

Psalm 37 Scripture for Memorization/Meditation

Delight yourself also in the Lord, and He shall give you the desires of your heart. Commit your way to the Lord. Trust also in Him, and He shall bring it to pass.
VERSES 4–5

The mouth of the righteous speaks wisdom, and his tongue speaks of justice. The law of his God is in his heart; none of his steps shall slide.
VERSES 30–31

Verses for Further Memorization/Meditation

- And those who know Your name will put their trust in You, for You, Lord, have not forsaken those who seek You (Psalm 9:10).
- "And all these blessings shall come on you and overtake you, if you listen to the voice of the Lord your God" (Deuteronomy 28:2).
- "But love your enemies, and do good, and lend, hoping for nothing back. And your reward shall be great, and you shall be the children of the Highest. For He is kind to the unthankful and to the evil" (Luke 6:35).
- The Lord your God in the midst of you is mighty. He will save; He will rejoice over you with joy. He will rest in His love; He will rejoice over you with singing (Zephaniah 3:17).

Study 12

PSALM 40

The Lord has answered David's prayer, and his personal difficulties pale in comparison with his joy. We see that David's patience has been rewarded. He has regained his spiritual footing.

When we stop long enough to ponder what God has done for us, we discover it's impossible to think of everything. Therefore, to envy proud and irreligious people, or to pursue false gods, is all the more foolish.

It isn't that David's problems are over. He still faces too many troubles to number. They continue to have a negative effect on him. Among his problems is the ongoing persecution from his enemies who want to take his life and in the meantime hound him verbally.

Psalm 40 Outline

(VERSES 1–3) Blessings in waiting patiently for the Lord

(VERSES 4–5) The God who thinks about His people

(VERSES 6–8) Delighting in obedience

(VERSES 9–12) Proclaiming God's praise

(VERSES 13–15) David's plea for God's deliverance and help

(VERSES 16–17) Praise and humble pleas

To the chief musician, a psalm of David.

[1]I waited patiently for the Lord, and He inclined to me and heard my cry.

[2]He brought me up also out of a horrible pit, out of the miry clay, and set my feet on a rock, and established my steps.

[3]And He has put a new song in my mouth, even praise to our God. Many shall see it and fear and shall trust in the Lord.

[4]Blessed is that man who makes the Lord his trust and does not respect the proud or those who turn aside to lies.

[5]Many, O Lord my God, are Your wonderful works, which You have done, and Your thoughts that are toward us. They cannot be counted in order to You. If I would declare and speak of them, they are more than can be counted.

[6]You did not desire sacrifice and offering. You have opened my ears. You have not required burnt offering and sin offering.

[7]Then I said, "Behold, I have come. In the volume of the book it is written of me:

[8]I delight to do Your will, O my God. Yes, Your law is within my heart."

[9]I have preached righteousness in the great congregation. Behold, I have not refrained my lips, O Lord, You know.

[10]I have not hidden Your righteousness within my heart. I have declared Your faithfulness and Your salvation. I have not concealed Your loving-kindness and Your truth from the great congregation.

[11]Do not withhold Your tender mercies from me, O Lord. Let Your loving-kindness and Your truth continually preserve me.

[12]For innumerable evils have surrounded me. My iniquities have taken hold of me, so that I am not able to look up; they are more than the hairs of my head. Therefore my heart fails me.

[13]Be pleased, O Lord, to deliver me. O Lord, hurry to help me.

[14]Let those who seek after my soul to destroy it be ashamed and confounded together; let those who wish me evil be driven backward and put to shame.

[15]Let those who say to me "Aha, aha!" be desolate as a reward for their shame.

[16]Let all those who seek You rejoice and be glad in You.

Let those who love Your salvation say continually, "The Lord is magnified."

[17]But I am poor and needy; yet the Lord thinks of me. You are my help and my deliverer; do not delay, O my God.

Observe

What were the results of David waiting patiently upon God?

....

....

....

....

....

What did the psalmist say about God in verse 5?

....

....

....

....

....

What are the things David asked God for in this psalm?

....

....

....

....

....

Interpret

What did David say about God's deliverance in this psalm?

What does that teach us about prayer?

In what ways does David respond to what God had done for him?

Apply

PSALM 40

What does it mean to you to "wait upon the Lord" and what makes it challenging?

How can you be intentional to make gratitude a bigger part of your prayer life?

What great things has God done in your life?

Psalm 40 Scriptures for Memorization/Meditation

I waited patiently for the LORD, and He inclined to me and heard my cry. He brought me up also out of a horrible pit, out of the miry clay, and set my feet on a rock, and established my steps.
VERSES 1–2

I have not hidden Your righteousness within my heart. I have declared Your faithfulness and Your salvation. I have not concealed Your loving-kindness and Your truth from the great congregation.
VERSE 10

Verses for Further Memorization/Meditation

- Therefore, I will look to the LORD. I will wait for the God of my salvation. My God will hear me (Micah 7:7).
- For this is the love of God, that we keep His commandments. And His commandments are not grievous (1 John 5:3).
- "Stand in the gate of the LORD's house, and proclaim this word there, and say, 'Hear the word of the LORD, all you of Judah, who enter in at these gates to worship the Lord'" (Jeremiah 7:2).
- Jesus said to them, "My food is to do the will of Him who sent Me and to finish His work" (John 4:34).

Study 13

PSALM 46

This psalm, with its focus on the power and sovereignty of God, is similar to some of David's previous psalms. But where David's psalms are often intensely personal, this one is written with the nation of Israel in mind. The nation may have been facing some troublesome situations, but the psalmist envisions catastrophes to the extreme. Even if the mountains are to fall and the oceans are to rise, God will be there with His people, and they need not fear. Therefore, the Lord will surely see them through lesser problems.

Those coming out of a long, dark, troubling time can often feel insecurity and fatigue. But God is there to help His people at any time of the day. God is our always-dependable refuge and strength.

Psalm 46 Outline

(VERSES 1–3)	God is greater than any crisis
(VERSES 4–6)	God's provision
(VERSE 7)	God is with us
(VERSES 8–9)	The mighty works of God
(VERSE 10)	Be still in God's presence
(VERSE 11)	Confidence in the Lord

To the chief musician for the sons of Korah, a song on alamoth.

1 God is our refuge and strength, a very present help in trouble.
2 Therefore we will not fear, though the earth is removed,
and though the mountains are carried into the midst of the sea,
3 though its waters roar and are troubled, though the mountains shake with its swelling. *Selah.*
4 There is a river, the streams of which shall make glad the
city of God, the holy place of the tabernacles of the Most High.
5 God is in the midst of her; she shall not be moved. God shall
help her and that right early.
6 The nations raged; the kingdoms were moved. He uttered
His voice; the earth melted.
7 The LORD of hosts is with us; the God of Jacob is our
refuge. *Selah.*
8 Come, behold the works of the LORD, what desolations He
has made on the earth.
9 He makes wars to cease to the ends of the earth. He breaks
the bow and cuts the spear in pieces. He burns the chariot in
the fire.
10 "Be still and know that I am God. I will be exalted among
the nations; I will be exalted in the earth."
11 The LORD of hosts is with us; the God of Jacob is our
refuge. *Selah.*

Observe

What character traits of God are most emphasized in Psalm 46?

According to the psalmist, what sustains the believer and keeps her from being overcome with fear?

What promises are made to the people of Israel?

PSALM 46

Interpret

According to verses 1 through 3, what does God provide for His people?

What key words in this psalm encourage believers to fully depend on the Lord in times of trouble?

What does it mean that God is our “refuge”?

Apply

How has your relationship with God helped you in times when life seemed out of control?

What are the specific attributes of God helping you "be still" in a particular situation in your life right now?

How does knowing that the Lord is always with you bring hope and help when you are going through difficult times?

Psalm 46 Scripture for Memorization/Meditation

"Be still and know that I am God. I will be exalted among the nations; I will be exalted in the earth."
VERSE 10

Verses for Further Memorization/Meditation

- "Have I not commanded you? Be strong and of good courage. Do not be afraid or be dismayed, for the LORD your God is with you wherever you go" (Joshua 1:9).
- But my God shall supply all your need according to His riches in glory by Christ Jesus (Philippians 4:19).
- Do not fret because of him who prospers in his way, because of the man who brings wicked schemes to pass (Psalm 37:7).
- "Do not fear, for I am with you. Do not be dismayed, for I am your God. I will strengthen you. Yes, I will help you. Yes, I will uphold you with My righteous right hand" (Isaiah 41:10).

Study 14

PSALM 51

Psalm 51 is one of seven often categorized as "penitential." Its deeply personal and confessional tone is explained in the introduction. David composed this psalm after the prophet Nathan confronted him about his sin with Bathsheba (2 Samuel 12:1–25).

Considering that the baby he had conceived was already born, it's clear that David has avoided God for many months. But when faced with the severity of his sin, his confession is unabashed. David makes no attempt to deny his sin or excuse his behavior. He readily admits that his actions were rebellious and sinful. Yet he is also confident that God is a source of mercy, unfailing love, compassion, and cleansing.

After God forgives him, David can again live in the joy and gladness that he has been missing. And after God has blotted out his terrible offense, then David can renew his heart for the Lord. He prays not only for a pure heart but also for a steadfast spirit and ongoing awareness of God's presence. After his grievous sin, he desires the joy of salvation and a renewal of his willingness to serve God.

Psalm 51 Outline

(VERSES 1–2) David's appeal to God's love and mercy

(VERSES 3–6) David's confession

(VERSES 7–12) David's prayer for forgiveness and restoration

(VERSES 13–17) David's promise to God

(VERSES 18–19) David's prayer for his people

To the chief musician, a psalm of David, when Nathan the prophet came to him, after he had gone in to Bathsheba.

1 Have mercy on me, O God, according to Your loving-kindness; according to the multitude of Your tender mercies, blot out my transgressions.

2 Wash me thoroughly from my iniquity, and cleanse me from my sin.

3 For I acknowledge my transgressions, and my sin is ever before me.

4 Against You, You only, have I sinned, and done this evil in Your sight, that You might be justified when You speak and be clear when You judge.

5 Behold, I was formed in iniquity, and in sin my mother conceived me.

6 Behold, You desire truth in the inner parts, and in the hidden part You shall make me to know wisdom.

7 Purify me with hyssop, and I shall be clean. Wash me, and I shall be whiter than snow.

8 Cause me to hear joy and gladness, that the bones that You have broken may rejoice.

9 Hide Your face from my sins and blot out all my iniquities.

10 Create in me a clean heart, O God, and renew a right spirit within me.

11 Do not cast me away from Your presence, and do not take Your Holy Spirit from me.

12 Restore to me the joy of Your salvation, and uphold me with Your free Spirit.

13 Then I will teach transgressors Your ways, and sinners shall be converted to You.

14 Deliver me from the guilt of bloodshed, O God, the God of my salvation, and my tongue shall sing aloud of Your righteousness.

15 O Lord, You open my lips, and my mouth shall declare Your praise.

16 For You do not desire sacrifice, or else I would give it. You do not delight in burnt offering.

17 The sacrifices of God are a broken spirit; a broken and a contrite heart, O God, You will not despise.

[18]Do good in Your good pleasure to Zion; build the walls of Jerusalem.

[19]Then You shall be pleased with the sacrifices of righteousness, with burnt offering and whole burnt offering. Then they shall offer bulls on Your altar.

Observe

According to verse 1, why is God merciful to sinners?

....

....

....

....

What terms describe the way God purifies us from sin?

....

....

....

....

....

What did David pray his confession of sin would lead to?

....

....

....

....

....

Interpret

What does Psalm 51 show us about true repentance?

What does David mean when he says, "I was formed in iniquity, and in sin my mother conceived me" (verse 5)?

How did David respond to being forgiven and cleansed?

Apply

How should you, or others you know, handle nagging guilt about past sins?

What do the first two verses of Psalm 51 suggest about the confidence you need to bring your sins to the Lord?

What did you learn about the true nature of God's forgiveness?

Psalm 51 Scripture for Memorization/Meditation

Hide Your face from my sins and blot out
all my iniquities. Create in me a clean heart,
O God, and renew a right spirit within me.
VERSES 9–10

Verses for Further Memorization/Meditation

- But God, who is rich in mercy, for His great love in which He loved us even when we were dead in sins, has made us alive together with Christ (by grace you are saved) (Ephesians 2:4–5).
- He who covers his sins shall not prosper, but whoever confesses and forsakes them shall have mercy (Proverbs 28:13).
- Blessed is he whose transgression is forgiven, whose sin is covered. Blessed is the man to whom the LORD does not impute iniquity, and in whose spirit there is no deceit (Psalm 32:1–2).
- "Come and let us return to the LORD. For He has torn, and He will heal us. He has wounded, and He will bind us up" (Hosea 6:1).

Study 15

PSALM 55

The introduction to this psalm does not provide specifics about the event that inspired it, but the psalm itself reveals a painful betrayal by someone who had been a close friend. David's appeal to God includes an account of both the treatment he is receiving from others and the turmoil it has created within him. He describes a progression from anguish, to fear and trembling, to horror.

In the wake of such emotional trauma, David cries out to God evening, morning, and midday. His regular prayer times are reminiscent of Daniel's faithfulness and commitment to pray three times a day (Daniel 6:10). We might say "morning, noon, and night," but David cites "evening and morning and at noon" because the Jewish day started at sundown.

His response—and advice to others—is wise and appropriate. Those who cast their concerns on God will not be disappointed. God will simultaneously take care of the righteous while short-circuiting the work (if not the lives) of the wicked.

Psalm 55 Outline

(VERSES 1–3) David's complaint about his troubles

(VERSES 4–8) David's fear and trembling

(VERSES 9–11) Asking God to destroy his oppressors

(VERSES 12–14) A friend's betrayal

(VERSE 15) Asking the Lord to take vengeance

(VERSES 16–19) Confidence in God during difficulty

(VERSES 20–21) A treacherous enemy

(VERSES 22–23) Leaving matters in God's hands

To the chief musician on neginoth, maskil, a psalm of David.

1Give ear to my prayer, O God, and do not hide Yourself from my supplication.

2Attend to me, and hear me. I mourn in my complaint and make a noise,

3because of the voice of the enemy, because of the oppression of the wicked, for they cast iniquity on me, and in wrath they hate me.

4My heart is greatly pained within me, and the terrors of death have fallen on me.

5Fearfulness and trembling have come on me, and horror has overwhelmed me.

6And I said, "Oh that I had wings like a dove! For then would I fly away and be at rest.

7Behold, then would I wander far away and remain in the wilderness. *Selah.*

8I would hasten my escape from the windy storm and tempest."

9Destroy, O Lord, and divide their tongues, for I have seen violence and strife in the city.

10Day and night they go around it on its walls. Mischief also and sorrow are in the midst of it.

11Wickedness is in the midst of it; deceit and guile do not depart from her streets.

12For it was not an enemy who reproached me; then I could have borne it. Nor was it he who hated me who magnified himself against me; then I would have hidden myself from him.

13But it was you, a man my equal, my guide, and my acquaintance.

14We took sweet counsel together and walked to the house of God in company.

15Let death seize them, and let them go down alive into hell, for wickedness is in their dwellings and among them.

16As for me, I will call on God, and the LORD shall save me.

17Evening and morning and at noon I will pray and cry aloud, and He shall hear my voice.

18He has delivered my soul in peace from the battle that was against me, for there were many with me.

[19]God shall hear and afflict them, even He who abides of old.
Selah. Because they do not change, therefore they do not fear God.
[20]He has put forth his hands against those who are at peace
with him; he has broken his covenant.
[21]The words of his mouth were smoother than butter, but
war was in his heart. His words were softer than oil, yet they
were drawn swords.
[22]Cast your burden on the LORD, and He shall sustain you; He
shall never allow the righteous to be moved.
[23]But You, O God, shall bring them down into the pit of
destruction. Murderous and deceitful men shall not live out half
their days, but I will trust in You.

Observe

What emotions did David feel when he wrote this psalm?

....

....

....

What did David ask God to do with his oppressors?

....

....

....

What did David do about/with the crisis he faced?

....

....

....

Interpret

What can we learn from David's responses to his own fear?

....

....

....

....

....

....

What did David want to do because he was afraid?

....

....

....

....

....

....

In what did David take confidence, even though he was afraid? (see verse 17)

....

....

....

....

....

....

....

Apply

When you are afraid, what is the best thing to do with your fear?

Do you believe it is a sin to feel fear? Why or why not?

What might keep you from honestly communicating with God about your fear?

Psalm 55 Scripture for Memorization/Meditation

Cast your burden on the LORD, and He shall sustain you;
He shall never allow the righteous to be moved.
VERSE 22

Verses for Further Memorization/Meditation

- For God has not given us the spirit of fear, but of power and of love and of a sound mind (2 Timothy 1:7).
- "But I say to you who hear: Love your enemies. Do good to those who hate you. Bless those who curse you, and pray for those who spitefully use you" (Luke 6:27–28).
- If it is possible, as much as it lies in you, live peaceably with all men (Romans 12:18).
- Do not avenge yourselves, dearly beloved, but rather give place to wrath, for it is written, "Vengeance is Mine. I will repay," says the Lord (Romans 12:19).

Study 16

PSALM 56

The superscription of Psalm 56—"To the chief musician on Jonath Elem Rechokim, michtam of David, when the Philistines took him in Gath"—provides a clue as to the source of the emotions David expresses in this psalm. Gath was a Philistine city where David went to hide while trying to avoid capture by King Saul.

Though he eventually made a tentative alliance with the king of Gath (1 Samuel 27:1–7), an earlier visit hadn't been so amiable. When the people identified him as the one who had killed Goliath and many more of their soldiers, he quickly became persona non grata and even began to fear for his life. To extricate himself from the situation, he feigned madness. The Philistines forced him out of the city but did not harm him (1 Samuel 21:10–22:1).

After asking God not to let his persecutors escape, David urges God to keep track of his sorrows. He asks God to put his tears into a bottle. In other words, if God is well aware of David's situation, he trusts that the Lord will act to restrain the influence of his enemies.

Psalm 56 Outline

(VERSES 1–2) Looking to the Lord in a time of danger

(VERSES 3–4) Trust in the midst of fear

(VERSES 5–7) Continuing danger

(VERSES 8–9) God sees David's suffering

(VERSES 10–11) Confidence in the Lord

(VERSES 12–13) Fulfilling vows

To the chief musician on Jonath Elem Rechokim, michtam of David, when the Philistines took him in Gath.

1 Be merciful to me, O God, for man would swallow me up; fighting daily he oppresses me.

2 My enemies would daily swallow me up, for they are many who fight against me, O Most High.

3 When I am afraid, I will trust in You.

4 In God (I will praise His word), in God I have put my trust; I will not fear what flesh can do to me.

5 Every day they distort my words; all their thoughts are against me for evil.

6 They gather themselves together; they hide themselves; they observe my steps when they wait for my soul.

7 Shall they escape by iniquity? In Your anger cast down the people, O God.

8 You count my wanderings; You put my tears into Your bottle. Are they not in Your book?

9 When I cry to You, then my enemies shall turn back. This I know, for God is for me.

10 In God (I will praise His word), in the LORD (I will praise His word),

11 in God I have put my trust; I will not be afraid of what man can do to me.

12 Your vows are on me, O God. I will render praises to You.

13 For You have delivered my soul from death. Will You not deliver my feet from falling, that I may walk before God in the light of the living?

Observe

What motivated David to write this psalm?

What were David's feelings about his situation?

How did David demonstrate his trust in the Lord?

Interpret

In what ways is David a good example for us in how he handled fear and stress?

....

....

....

....

....

In light of this psalm, how should we change the way we deal with life's challenges?

....

....

....

....

....

....

What expectations can we confidently have of the Lord when we go to Him with our problems?

....

....

....

....

....

....

Apply

What have you learned about God's goodness from enduring difficult times in the past?

What usually motivates you to go to the Lord in prayer?

How can you best demonstrate your trust that God will move in your circumstances?

Psalm 56 Scripture for Memorization/Meditation

In God (I will praise His word), in God I have put my trust; I will not fear what flesh can do to me.
VERSE 4

Verses for Further Memorization/Meditation

- So we may boldly say, "The Lord is my helper, and I will not fear what man shall do to me" (Hebrews 13:6).
- And not only so, but we also glory in tribulations, knowing that tribulation works patience, and patience experience, and experience hope. And hope does not make us ashamed, because the love of God has been poured out in our hearts by the Holy Spirit who was given to us (Romans 5:3–5).
- And we know that all things work together for good for those who love God, for those who are called according to His purpose (Romans 8:28).
- When you make a vow to God, do not put off paying it, for He has no pleasure in fools. Pay what you have vowed. It is better that you should not vow than that you should vow and not pay (Ecclesiastes 5:4–5).

Study 17

PSALM 57

David wrote Psalm 57 as he attempted to evade the jealous and murderous king Saul (1 Samuel 19:1–2; 22:1; 24:2–3). He fled from pursuing attackers and hid in caves during this difficult time in his life.

This psalm is in two parts. Verses 1–5 depict David asking God to show him "mercy" and to save him from Saul. Verses 6–11 feature him thanking the Lord for saving him.

David expects to awaken at dawn with a steadfast heart and a song on his lips. He is eager to praise God and declare to other nations and peoples what God has done for him. God's love and faithfulness are unlimited, reaching to the heavens.

Psalm 57 Outline

(VERSES 1–3)	Trusting in the merciful God
(VERSE 4)	Dangerous enemies
(VERSE 5)	David exalts God
(VERSE 6)	The enemy's trap
(VERSES 7–10)	David's steadfast heart
(VERSE 11)	God-exalting words

To the chief musician, Al-tashheth, michtam of David, when he fled from Saul in the cave.

1 Be merciful to me, O God, be merciful to me, for my soul trusts
in You. Yes, in the shadow of Your wings I will make my refuge,
until these calamities have passed.
2 I will cry to God Most High, to God who performs all
things for me.
3 He shall send from heaven and save me from the reproach
of him who would swallow me up. *Selah*. God shall send forth
His mercy and His truth.
4 My soul is among lions, and I lie even among those who are
set on fire, even the sons of men, whose teeth are spears and
arrows, and their tongue a sharp sword.
5 Be exalted, O God, above the heavens; let Your glory be
above all the earth.
6 They have prepared a net for my steps; my soul is bowed
down. They have dug a pit before me, into the midst of which
they have fallen themselves. *Selah*.
7 My heart is steadfast, O God, my heart is steadfast. I will
sing and give praise.
8 Awake, my glory! Awake, lyre and harp! I myself will
wake up early.
9 I will praise You, O Lord, among the people. I will sing to You
among the nations.
10 For Your mercy is great to the heavens, and Your truth to
the clouds.
11 Be exalted, O God, above the heavens. Let Your glory be
above all the earth.

Observe

How did David describe his predicament?

How did David deal with the challenge he faced?

What did David expect from the Lord?

Interpret

What kind of relationship did David have with God?

....

....

....

....

....

....

How did David describe God's character in Psalm 57?

....

....

....

....

....

....

What do David's words reveal about his motives in asking God for help?

....

....

....

....

....

....

....

Apply

How can you show your thankfulness to God for the ways He has helped you in life?

What are some practical ways to prepare yourself to face opposition or temptation?

When you feel insecure or scared, how can you follow David's example to find comfort?

Psalm 57 Scripture for Memorization/Meditation

Be exalted, O God, above the heavens.
Let Your glory be above all the earth.
VERSE 11

Verses for Further Memorization/Meditation

- And the Lord passed by before him and proclaimed, "The Lord, the Lord God, merciful and gracious, longsuffering, and abundant in goodness and truth" (Exodus 34:6).
- Bless those who persecute you. Bless, and do not curse (Romans 12:14).
- Forever, O Lord, Your word is settled in heaven. Your faithfulness is to all generations; You have established the earth, and it abides (Psalm 119:89–90).
- Therefore, my beloved brothers, be steadfast, immovable, always abounding in the work of the Lord, since you know that your labor is not in vain in the Lord (1 Corinthians 15:58).

Study 18

PSALM 62

The fact that this psalm makes the observation that opponents are attempting to cast down the psalmist suggests that it is authored by a king (presumed to be David). A king has many resources at his disposal, yet David's sole source of help and comfort is God. God is his security (rock), deliverance (salvation), and protection (stronghold). Humanity, on the other hand, is a continual source of chaos.

People have repeatedly attempted to undermine David. The assaults of others are verbal as well. They bless him to his face but curse him and tell lies about him behind his back. They do not rest from their efforts to put him down.

The psalmist's description of human beings is in direct contrast to his image of God. The Lord is a rock and fortress; people are nothing. Even those who perceive themselves as wealthy and entitled will soon be deflated and forgotten.

Psalm 62 Outline

(VERSES 1–2) Silently waiting for God

(VERSES 3–4) David's enemies

(VERSES 5–7) Confidence in the Lord alone

(VERSES 8–10) Trusting in God, not others

(VERSES 11–12) Learning of God's power and mercy

To the chief musician, to Jeduthun, a psalm of David.

1 Truly my soul waits for God; from Him comes my salvation.

2 He alone is my rock and my salvation. He is my defense; I shall not be greatly moved.

3 How long will you devise mischief against a man? You shall be slain, all of you; as a bowing wall you shall be, and as a tottering fence.

4 They only consult to cast him down from his excellency; they delight in lies. They bless with their mouth, but they curse inwardly. *Selah.*

5 My soul, wait for God alone, for my expectation is from Him.

6 He alone is my rock and my salvation. He is my defense; I shall not be moved.

7 In God is my salvation and my glory; the rock of my strength, and my refuge, is in God.

8 Trust in Him at all times. You people, pour out your heart before Him. God is a refuge for us. *Selah.*

9 Surely men of low degree are a breath, and men of high degree are a lie; to be laid in the balance, they are altogether lighter than breath.

10 Do not trust in oppression, and do not become vain in robbery. If riches increase, do not set your heart on them.

11 God has spoken once; twice have I heard this: that power belongs to God.

12 Also to You, O Lord, belongs mercy, for You render to every man according to his work.

Observe

How did David demonstrate his confidence in God in the face of danger?

How did David reveal his feelings of insecurity in his own strength?

How did David advise God's people to pray?

Interpret

Which of God's characteristics encourage His people to rely on Him?

How did the writer offer reassurance to trust in the Lord?

What encouragement did the psalmist give to God's people?

How can you best serve God with the riches He has given to you?

Why can you put your confidence and faith in God?

Which of God's characteristics encourages you to rely on Him rather than on yourself?

Psalm 62 Scripture for Memorization/Meditation

Trust in Him at all times. You people, pour out your heart before Him. God is a refuge for us.
VERSE 8

Verses for Further Memorization/Meditation

- The LORD is good to those who wait for Him, to the soul who seeks Him. It is good that a man should both hope and quietly wait for the salvation of the LORD (Lamentations 3:25–26).
- "Behold, God is my salvation. I will trust and not be afraid, 'for the LORD JEHOVAH is my strength and my song. He also has become my salvation'" (Isaiah 12:2).
- And this is the confidence that we have in Him, that if we ask anything according to His will, He hears us (1 John 5:14).
- Now may the God of hope fill you with all joy and peace in believing, that you may abound in hope through the power of the Holy Spirit (Romans 15:13).

Study 19
PSALM 67

Psalm 67, crafted by an unknown writer, is a group prayer request for God's favor. The opening verses reflect the blessing taught to the priests in Numbers 6:24–26: "The LORD bless you and keep you. The LORD make His face shine on you and be gracious to you. The LORD lift up His countenance on you and give you peace."

In this psalm, the people of Israel not only sing their request that God would bless them, but they ask the Lord to bless the Gentiles they encounter. This is a beautiful example of God's people asking that He would spread His salvation and praise around the world.

Psalm 67 Outline

(VERSE 1)	A request for mercy, blessing, and God's presence
(VERSE 2)	Proper motivation for prayer requests
(VERSE 3)	A prayer for all peoples
(VERSES 4–5)	Joyful anticipation
(VERSE 6–7)	Answers to prayer

To the chief musician on neginoth, a psalm or song.

1God be merciful to us and bless us and cause His face to shine
on us, *Selah*.
2that Your way may be known on earth, Your saving health
among all nations.
3Let the people praise You, O God; let all the people praise You.
4O let the nations be glad and sing for joy, for You shall judge
the people righteously and govern the nations on earth. *Selah*.
5Let the people praise You, O God; let all the people praise You.
6Then the earth shall yield her increase, and God, even our
own God, shall bless us.
7God shall bless us, and all the ends of the earth shall fear Him.

Observe

What are the recurring terms and themes in this psalm?

Why did the writer want the Lord to bless him and his people?

How did people speaking this psalm seek to move God to answer their prayer?

Interpret

How should all people respond to God's guidance?

What results did the psalm writer expect to see from this prayer?

In what ways should we follow the writer's example in asking for God's blessings?

Apply

Looking at every part of your life, where do you most want the Lord to "make His face shine on" you?

....

....

....

....

....

....

What is the best attitude to have as you pray?

....

....

....

....

....

....

How do your motives matter when going to God in prayer?

....

....

....

....

....

....

....

Psalm 67 Scripture for Memorization/Meditation

Let the people praise You, O God; let all the people praise You.
VERSE 3

Verses for Further Memorization/Meditation

- I exhort therefore, first of all, that supplications, prayers, intercessions, and giving of thanks be made for all men, for kings and for all who are in authority, that we may lead a quiet and peaceful life in all godliness and honesty (1 Timothy 2:1–2).
- Draw near to God and He will draw near to you. Cleanse your hands, you sinners, and purify your hearts, you double-minded (James 4:8).
- "Therefore, pray according to this manner: Our Father who is in heaven, hallowed be Your name. Your kingdom come. Your will be done on earth as it is in heaven. Give us this day our daily bread. And forgive us our debts, as we forgive our debtors. And do not lead us into temptation, but deliver us from evil. For Yours is the kingdom and the power and the glory forever. Amen" (Matthew 6:9–13).
- And whatever we ask we receive from Him, because we keep His commandments and do those things that are pleasing in His sight (1 John 3:22).

Study 20

PSALM 84

A rich and rewarding relationship with God helps to change one's perspective on life. Psalm 84 is the psalmist's expression of longing to be closer to God and to *remain* close. The opening verses appear to focus on the temple building with its courtyards. By the end of the psalm, however, it becomes clear that it is the presence of God Himself that the writer desires most.

Being in His presence at His temple is akin to standing in the brightness of the sun, yet being shielded and protected at the same time. To those who can stand before Him blameless, God will grant blessing and deny nothing good. Trust in God, however, is essential in receiving what He has to offer.

Psalm 84 Outline

(VERSES 1–2) Longing for God and for His house

(VERSES 3–4) Blessings and satisfaction in the house of God

(VERSES 5–7) Strength in the Lord

(VERSES 8–9) Seeking God's attention

(VERSES 10–12) God's greatness

To the chief musician on gittith, a psalm for the sons of Korah.

[1]How lovely are Your tabernacles, O LORD of hosts!
[2]My soul longs, yes, even faints for the courts of the LORD.
My heart and my flesh cry out for the living God.
[3]Yes, the sparrow has found a house, and the swallow a nest
for herself, where she may lay her young, even Your altars, O
LORD of hosts, my King, and my God.
[4]Blessed are those who dwell in Your house; they will still be
praising You. *Selah.*
[5]Blessed is the man whose strength is in You, in whose heart
are the roads to them,
[6]who passing through the Valley of Baca make it a well; the
rain also fills the pools.
[7]They go from strength to strength; every one of them in
Zion appears before God.
[8]O LORD God of hosts, hear my prayer. Give ear, O God of
Jacob. *Selah.*
[9]Behold, O God our shield, and look at the face of Your anointed.
[10]For a day in Your courts is better than a thousand. I would
rather be a doorkeeper in the house of my God than dwell in the
tents of wickedness.
[11]For the LORD God is a sun and shield. The LORD will give
grace and glory; no good thing will He withhold from those who
walk uprightly.
[12]O LORD of hosts, blessed is the man who trusts in You.

Observe

What is the main theme of Psalm 84?

To what does the psalmist liken the Lord?

How does the psalmist express his love for God?

Interpret

What do you think the psalmist meant when he used the phrase "go from strength to strength"?

What might the writer be suggesting when he wrote that God is "a sun"?

From whom will the Lord "not withhold any good thing"?

Can you remember a time when you sensed that God was your shield?

Has there been a moment where you sensed that God was your sun?

Why is it important for you to go to church and worship God?

PSALM 84

Psalm 84 Scripture for Memorization/Meditation

My soul longs, yes, even faints for the courts of the Lord.
My heart and my flesh cry out for the living God.
verse 2

Verses for Further Memorization/Meditation

- "Yours, O Lord, is the greatness and the power and the glory and the victory and the majesty, for all that is in heaven and on the earth is Yours. Yours is the kingdom, O Lord, and You are exalted as head above all" (1 Chronicles 29:11).
- Hear the just, O Lord; attend to my cry. Give ear to my prayer that does not go out from deceitful lips (Psalm 17:1).
- As the deer pants for the water brooks, so my soul pants for You, O God. My soul thirsts for God, for the living God. When shall I come and appear before God? (Psalm 42:1–2).
- Whom have I in heaven but You? And there is none on earth that I desire besides You (Psalm 73:25).

Study 21

PSALM 86

While many of the psalms are appeals to God on a national level, Psalm 86 is the prayer of an individual concerning his personal troubles. David expresses his general state of mind. He is poor and needy, but the specifics of his situation aren't revealed until later. First, he wants to appeal to God for mercy and protection. David's trust is in God and he is quick to seek help, but his current situation has robbed him of joy. He is counting on God's love and forgiveness, fully expecting an answer.

David desires instruction from God. He wants to know truth and to cultivate an undivided heart. God has loved him and delivered him, and he wants to praise and glorify the Lord as a result. Only then does David get to the crux of the matter: He is being personally attacked by numerous unrighteous people who want his life. But his specific complaint doesn't matter; he has already entrusted himself to God, so the nature of the problem is inconsequential. God can handle it.

Psalm 86 Outline

(VERSE 1)	A needy person's plea for help
(VERSE 2)	Why God hears David's prayer
(VERSES 3–4)	David cries out to God for mercy
(VERSE 5)	Relying on God's graciousness
(VERSES 6–7)	David's confidence in the Lord
(VERSES 8–10)	God's greatness
(VERSES 11–12)	Complete dependence on a great God
(VERSES 13–15)	The dependable graciousness of God
(VERSES 16–17)	David's plea for help

A prayer of David.

1 Bow down Your ear, O LORD; hear me, for I am poor and needy.

2 Preserve my soul, for I am holy. O You, my God, save Your servant who trusts in You.

3 Be merciful to me, O Lord, for I cry to You daily.

4 Rejoice the soul of Your servant, for to You, O Lord, I lift up my soul.

5 For You, Lord, are good, and ready to forgive, and abundant in mercy to all those who call on You.

6 Give ear, O LORD, to my prayer, and attend to the voice of my supplications.

7 In the day of my trouble I will call on You, for You will answer me.

8 Among the gods there is none like You, O Lord, nor are there any works like Your works.

9 All nations whom You have made shall come and worship before You, O Lord, and shall glorify Your name.

10 For You are great and do wondrous things. You are God alone.

11 Teach me Your way, O LORD; I will walk in Your truth. Unite my heart to fear Your name.

12 I will praise You, O Lord my God, with all my heart, and I will glorify Your name forevermore.

13 For great is Your mercy toward me, and You have delivered my soul from the lowest hell.

14 O God, the proud have risen against me, and the assemblies of violent men have sought after my soul and have not set You before them.

15 But You, O Lord, are a God full of compassion, and gracious, long-suffering, and abundant in mercy and truth.

16 O turn to me and have mercy on me; give Your strength to Your servant, and save the son of Your handmaiden.

17 Show me a token for good, that those who hate me may see it and be ashamed, because You, LORD, have helped me and comforted me.

Observe

What was David's difficulty?

What blessings did he seek from the Lord?

How did David demonstrate his dependence on God?

PSALM 86

Interpret

What does this psalm reveal about David's relationship with God?

Why was he confident that the Lord would answer his prayer?

What other sources of help did David have?

How can you make your relationship with God more like David's?

What are ways that you could remind yourself every day of God's faithfulness, mercy, and love?

How are you challenged to pray differently today?

Psalm 86 Scripture for Memorization/Meditation

Give ear, O Lord, to my prayer, and attend to the voice of my supplications. In the day of my trouble I will call on You, for You will answer me.
verses 6–7

Verses for Further Memorization/Meditation

- In my distress I called on the Lord and cried to my God. He heard my voice out of His temple, and my cry came before Him, even into His ears (Psalm 18:6).
- "Then you shall call on Me and you shall go and pray to Me, and I will listen to you. And you shall seek Me and find Me, when you search for Me with all your heart" (Jeremiah 29:12–13).
- Confess your faults to one another and pray for one another, that you may be healed. The effective fervent prayer of a righteous man avails much (James 5:16).
- The angel of the Lord encamps around those who fear him and delivers them (Psalm 34:7).

Study 22
PSALM 91

This psalm begins by using most laudable names for God: *Most High* and *Almighty*. In doing so, the psalmist provides the reason why we can feel secure, even during times of trouble. Rather than using first person to speak only of his own experiences, he uses third person to indicate that the comforting protection of God is available to anyone willing to seek God's guidance.

It is critical to take refuge in God—it's what makes the difference between security and susceptibility to danger. No ultimate harm will befall someone who takes refuge in the mighty God.

Psalm 91 Outline

(VERSES 1–2)	The protection and comfort the Lord provides
(VERSES 3–4)	Delivered and covered
(VERSES 5–6)	Delivered from fear
(VERSES 7–8)	Assurance for those who depend on the Lord
(VERSES 9–13)	Deliverance and assurance of victory
(VERSES 14–16)	Promises of blessing to the one who loves the Lord

1 He who dwells in the secret place of the Most High shall abide
under the shadow of the Almighty.
2 I will say of the LORD, “He is my refuge and my fortress. My
God, in Him I will trust.”
3 Surely He shall deliver you from the snare of the fowler and
from the dangerous pestilence.
4 He shall cover you with His feathers, and under His wings
you shall trust. His truth shall be your shield and buckler.
5 You shall not be afraid of the terror by night, or of the arrow
that flies by day,
6 or of the pestilence that walks in darkness, or of the destruction that wastes at noonday.
7 A thousand shall fall at your side, and ten thousand at your
right hand, but it shall not come near you.
8 Only with your eyes you shall look and see the reward of
the wicked.
9 Because you have made the LORD, who is my refuge, even
the Most High, your habitation,
10 no evil shall befall you, nor shall any plague come near
your dwelling.
11 For He shall give His angels charge over you, to guard you
in all your ways.
12 They shall lift you up in their hands, lest you dash your
foot against a stone.
13 You shall tread on the lion and adder; you shall trample the
young lion and the dragon underfoot.
14 “Because he has set his love on Me, therefore will I deliver
him. I will set him on high, because he has known My name.
15 He shall call on Me, and I will answer him. I will be with him
in trouble; I will deliver him and honor him.
16 I will satisfy him with long life and show him My salvation.”

Observe

What is the main theme of this psalm?

In verses 1–2, what four names for God are used?

From what does the psalmist say God will rescue him?

Interpret

What does it mean to dwell in the shelter of the Most High?

Why does the psalmist feel secure from danger?

What gives him confidence that he has a secure refuge in the Lord?

What difficulties are you facing right now that you can trust God to help you with?

How does choosing to trust the Lord change how you will approach these challenges ?

In what ways do you see God as your refuge?

Psalm 91 Scripture for Memorization/Meditation

He who dwells in the secret place of the Most High
shall abide under the shadow of the Almighty.
VERSE 1

Verses for Further Memorization/Meditation

- And Miriam answered them: "Sing to the LORD, for He has triumphed gloriously. The horse and his rider He has thrown into the sea" (Exodus 15:21).
- Lord, You have been our dwelling place in all generations (Psalm 90:1).
- "No weapon that is formed against you shall prosper, and you shall condemn every tongue that rises against you in judgment. This is the heritage of the servants of the LORD, and their righteousness is from Me," says the LORD (Isaiah 54:17).
- But the Lord is faithful, who shall establish you and keep you from evil (2 Thessalonians 3:3).

Study 23

PSALM 116

The book of Psalms, as well as the rest of the Bible, gives many reasons to love God. The reason cited in Psalm 116 is God's protection during a difficult time in the psalmist's life. The writer had cried out for the mercy of God, and the Lord responded.

The psalmist is eager to repay the Lord for His goodness. He has been delivered, so he will worship God publicly and intently. The cup of salvation may have been a drink offering (Numbers 28:7, 10, 14, 31) to accompany the psalmist's thank offering. Even though he has been spared from death this time, he knows that God is well aware of the deaths of His faithful followers. After his recovery, the psalmist intends to gladly continue to fulfill his vows to God, setting a good example for everyone.

Psalm 116 Outline

(VERSES 1–2) The God who hears prayer

(VERSES 3–4) Prayers of sorrow

(VERSES 5–7) The God who preserves us

(VERSES 8–11) Praise from the mouth of the one delivered

(VERSES 12–14) Receiving and responding to God's blessings

(VERSES 15–18) A grateful pledge

1 I love the Lord because He has heard my voice and my supplications.

2 Because He has inclined His ear to me, therefore I will call on Him as long as I live.

3 The sorrows of death surrounded me, and the pains of hell took hold of me. I found trouble and sorrow.

4 Then I called on the name of the Lord: "O Lord, I beg You, deliver my soul."

5 Gracious is the Lord, and righteous; yes, our God is merciful.

6 The Lord preserves the simple. I was brought low, and He helped me.

7 Return to your rest, O my soul, for the Lord has dealt bountifully with you.

8 For You have delivered my soul from death, my eyes from tears, and my feet from falling.

9 I will walk before the Lord in the land of the living.

10 I believed; therefore I said, "I was greatly afflicted."

11 I said in my haste, "All men are liars."

12 What shall I repay to the Lord for all His benefits toward me?

13 I will take the cup of salvation and call on the name of the Lord.

14 I will pay my vows to the Lord now in the presence of all His people.

15 Precious in the sight of the Lord is the death of His saints.

16 O Lord, truly I am Your servant; I am Your servant and the son of Your handmaiden. You have released me from my chains.

17 I will offer to You the sacrifice of thanksgiving and will call on the name of the Lord.

18 I will pay my vows to the Lord now in the presence of all His people,

19 in the courts of the Lord's house, in the midst of you, O Jerusalem. Praise the Lord.

Observe

What is the focus of the psalmist's praise?

How had God met his needs?

From what difficulty had God delivered the writer?

Interpret

Why did the writer depend so fully on God?

What were his feelings about the Lord?

What does this psalm reveal about the psalmist's faith?

Apply

What can you learn about gratitude from this psalm?

....

....

....

....

....

....

In what ways have you benefited from God's faithfulness in the past?

....

....

....

....

....

....

What are some key truths you can learn from this psalm about worshipping the Lord?

....

....

....

....

....

....

Psalm 116 Scripture for Memorization/Meditation

I will offer to You the sacrifice of thanksgiving
and will call on the name of the Lord.
verse 17

Verses for Further Memorization/Meditation

- "Call to Me, and I will answer you and show you great and mighty things that you do not know" (Jeremiah 33:3).
- Therefore if any man is in Christ, he is a new creature. Old things have passed away; behold, all things have become new (2 Corinthians 5:17).
- For His anger endures but a moment; in His favor is life. Weeping may endure for a night, but joy comes in the morning (Psalm 30:5).
- He shall redeem their soul from deceit and violence, and their blood shall be precious in His sight (Psalm 72:14).

Study 24

PSALM 120

Psalms 120–134 are identified as Songs of Degrees, or Songs of Ascents, a title that is not clear. The Jewish Mishna associates the fifteen psalms with the fifteen steps that led to the temple, where the Levites who led the music would sing

In this particular psalm, the writer stated the cause of his distress—evil, deceitful words spoken against him. He took some comfort in knowing that the evil spoken against him was untrue and that the Lord heard him when he cried out to his God.

The psalmist gave voice to his firm conviction that He heard and would answer his prayer. In doing that, he set an example we can all follow when we go to the Lord in prayer.

Psalm 120 Outline

(VERSES 1–2)	God's deliverance from distress
(VERSES 3–4)	The destiny of the deceitful
(VERSES 5–6)	Living with those who hate God's peace
(VERSE 7)	The contrast between the singer and the people he lives among

A song of degrees.

[1]In my distress, I cried to the Lord, and He heard me.
[2]Deliver my soul, O Lord, from lying lips and from a deceitful tongue.
[3]What shall be given to you? Or what shall be done to you,
you false tongue?
[4]Sharp arrows of the mighty, with coals of juniper.
[5]Woe is me, that I sojourn in Meshech, that I dwell in the
tents of Kedar!
[6]My soul has long dwelled with him who hates peace.
[7]I am for peace, but when I speak, they are for war.

Observe

What does the writer say about how God will ultimately handle this world's evil?

What is the most important theme of Psalm 120?

Why is the psalmist distressed?

PSALM 120

Interpret

How do those who follow God differ from those who don't?

What were the psalm writer's felt needs?

What does this psalm tell us about feeling alone?

Apply

PSALM 120

When have you felt the need to cry out to God for help and hope?

How has doing this changed your heart and mind?

How would you respond if God put you in a place where you didn't feel accepted or appreciated?

Psalm 120 Scripture for Memorization/Meditation

In my distress, I cried to the LORD, and He heard me.
VERSE 1

Verses for Further Memorization/Meditation

- . . .above all, taking the shield of faith, with which you shall be able to quench all the fiery darts of the wicked (Ephesians 6:16).
- But rejoice because you are partakers of Christ's sufferings, that when His glory shall be revealed you may be glad also with exceeding joy (1 Peter 4:13).
- And do not be conformed to this world, but be transformed by the renewing of your mind, that you may prove what is that good and acceptable and perfect will of God (Romans 12:2).
- Do not love the world or the things that are in the world. If any man loves the world, the love of the Father is not in him. For all that is in the world—the lust of the flesh, and the lust of the eyes, and the pride of life—is not of the Father but is of the world (1 John 2:15–16).

Study 25

PSALM 121

Psalm 121 confidently celebrates the Creator's very personal care for His people. The Israelites used this short psalm to focus their thoughts on the Lord as they traveled to Jerusalem.

Like the Israelites, we can comfort ourselves in the Lord, particularly when we face great difficulties and dangers. God's protection is like shade in the hot and sometimes hostile climate of the Middle East. It was also thought at the time that too much exposure to the moon could cause problems as well. (English words such as *moonstruck* and *lunatic* are examples of such a belief.) But God's protection works day and night. In addition, God will watch the pilgrim for the roundtrip—coming *and* going.

Psalm 121 Outline

(VERSES 1–2) Our help comes from the Lord our Creator

(VERSES 3–4) The nature of God's help

(VERSES 5–6) The Lord brings help around the clock

(VERSES 7–8) God preserves His people from evil

A song of degrees.

1I will lift up my eyes to the hills. Where does my help come from?
2My help comes from the LORD, who made heaven and earth.
3He will not allow your foot to be moved; He who keeps you will not slumber.
4Behold, He who keeps Israel shall neither slumber nor sleep.
5The LORD is your keeper. The LORD is your shade on your right hand.
6The sun shall not strike you by day, nor the moon by night.
7The LORD shall preserve you from all evil; He shall preserve your soul.
8The LORD shall preserve your going out and your coming in from this time forth, and even forevermore.

Observe

What does Psalm 121 reveal about the Lord's character and ways?

What did the writer of this psalm need from God?

What specific words reveal the benefits of looking to the Lord first for help?

PSALM 121

Interpret

What did the psalmist mean when he wrote, "The Lord is your shade on your right hand"?

What does verse 6 suggest about God's dependability?

If we believe that the Lord "made heaven and earth," how should we view Him?

Apply

How does this psalm help shape your understanding of the way God relates to you?

How have you benefited from God watching over you in the past?

What do you do when the battles feel overwhelming and you need God's protection?

Psalm 121 Scripture for Memorization/Meditation

The Lord shall preserve you from all evil;
He shall preserve your soul.
VERSE 7

Verses for Further Memorization/Meditation

- Behold, God is my helper; the Lord is with those who uphold my soul (Psalm 54:4).
- You are my hiding place. You shall preserve me from trouble. You shall surround me with songs of deliverance. *Selah* (Psalm 32:7).
- God is our refuge and strength, a very present help in trouble (Psalm 46:1).
- "And do not lead us into temptation, but deliver us from evil" (Matthew 6:13).

Study 26

PSALM 127

The first part of Psalm 127 points out futility of working without considering God's truth, God's will, God's approval, or God's wisdom. Without those things, even the most focused human effort is pointless. Jesus delivered this same message in Matthew 7:24–27.

People should acknowledge their children as blessings of God, not merely products of their own biological design. In ancient culture, sons were especially valued. As male children grew, they provided help on the farms, protection against danger, and representation of the family. The more sons parents produced, the more they felt that God had blessed them.

Psalm 127 Outline

(VERSE 1)	The Lord's work of building and guarding
(VERSE 2)	The vanity of relying on human strength or effort
(VERSE 3)	The blessings of children
(VERSES 4–5)	Likening children to arrows

A song of degrees for Solomon.

1Unless the LORD builds the house, those who build it labor in
vain. Unless the LORD keeps the city, the watchman wakes in vain.
2It is useless for you to rise up early, to sit up late, to eat the
bread of sorrows, for so He gives His beloved sleep.
3Behold, children are a heritage from the LORD, and the fruit
of the womb is His reward.
4Like arrows in the hand of a mighty man, so are children of
the youth.
5Happy is the man who has his quiver full of them. They shall
not be ashamed, but they shall speak with the enemies in the gate.

Observe

What are the repeated words and ideas in Psalm 127?

What do we learn about God from this psalm?

What promises are made?

Interpret

What does the phrase "in vain" mean in this psalm?

How should Psalm 127 shape our view of work?

What does it say about how God sees children?

As you read, what did you learn about yourself and how God relates to you?

In what ways do you find yourself relying on your own strength?

How can you fight the temptation to rely on yourself and instead rely on the Lord?

Psalm 127 Scripture for Memorization/Meditation

Unless the LORD builds the house, those who build it labor in vain. Unless the LORD keeps the city, the watchman wakes in vain.
VERSE 1

Verses for Further Memorization/Meditation

- For by grace you are saved through faith, and that is not of yourselves; it is the gift of God, not of works, lest any man should boast (Ephesians 2:8–9).
- Then I looked at all the works that my hands had done, and on the labor that I had labored to do, and behold, all was vanity and vexation of spirit, and there was no profit under the sun (Ecclesiastes 2:11).
- “Truly I say to you, whoever shall not receive the kingdom of God as a little child, he shall not enter in it” (Mark 10:15).
- And you, fathers, do not provoke your children to wrath, but bring them up in the nurture and admonition of the Lord (Ephesians 6:4).

Study 27

PSALM 136

It seems clear from the structure of Psalm 136 that it was used for public worship. A designated Levite recited the first portion of each statement as a temple choir, or perhaps the worshippers in attendance, responded with, "for His mercy endures forever." Like Psalm 135, this psalm begins with the affirmation that God is good and then details ways to praise Him for His greatness. He is God of gods and Lord of lords. With these initial observations, the accompanying triple command to give thanks in the first three verses is an emphatic opening.

This psalm ends by acknowledging the ongoing work of God. He never forgot His people when they were suffering. He had always delivered them from their enemies. He provided food and necessities, and His provision went beyond Israel. God had been Creator of the world, and His gifts were available to every living thing. There are many reasons to give thanks to God. But at the top of the list, as the psalmist reminds his listeners twenty-six times during this song, God should be thanked because His mercy endures forever.

Psalm 136 Outline

(VERSES 1–4) The God of goodness and mercy

(VERSES 5–9) God's enduring mercy

(VERSES 10–15) Deliverance from Egypt

(VERSES 16–22) God's mercy from the wilderness to the promised land

(VERSES 23–25) God's ongoing deliverance and help

(VERSE 26) Gratitude for God's enduring mercy

1 O give thanks to the LORD, for He is good, for His mercy
endures forever.
2 O give thanks to the God of gods, for His mercy endures forever.
3 O give thanks to the Lord of lords, for His mercy
endures forever;
4 to Him who alone does great wonders, for His mercy
endures forever;
5 to Him who by wisdom made the heavens, for His mercy
endures forever;
6 to Him who stretched out the earth above the waters, for
His mercy endures forever;
7 to Him who made great lights, for His mercy endures forever;
8 the sun to rule by day, for His mercy endures forever;
9 the moon and stars to rule by night, for His mercy
endures forever;
10 to Him who struck Egypt in their firstborn, for His mercy
endures forever;
11 and brought Israel out from among them, for His mercy
endures forever;
12 with a strong hand and with an outstretched arm, for His
mercy endures forever;
13 to Him who divided the Red Sea into parts, for His mercy
endures forever;
14 and made Israel to pass through the midst of it, for His
mercy endures forever;
15 but overthrew Pharaoh and his army in the Red Sea, for
His mercy endures forever;
16 to Him who led His people through the wilderness, for His
mercy endures forever;
17 to Him who struck great kings, for His mercy endures forever;
18 and slew famous kings, for His mercy endures forever:
19 Sihon, king of the Amorites, for His mercy endures forever;
20 and Og, the king of Bashan, for His mercy endures forever;
21 and gave their land as a heritage, for His mercy
endures forever;
22 even a heritage to Israel His servant, for His mercy
endures forever;

23who remembered us in our lowly condition, for His mercy endures forever;
24and has redeemed us from our enemies, for His mercy endures forever;
25who gives food to all flesh, for His mercy endures forever.
26O give thanks to the God of heaven, for His mercy endures forever.

Observe

What does the psalmist state about the Lord in verses 1–4?

What events of Old Testament history are recounted in this psalm?

What is the writer's response to God's goodness and mercy?

Interpret

What is the overriding message of Psalm 136?

What does it mean to say God's "mercy endures forever"?

What does this psalm reveal about the Lord's true character?

Apply

How does it encourage you to know that God's love and mercy will never end?

In what specific ways have you seen God's mighty hand at work in your life?

How can you remind yourself daily of all the good things God has done for you?

Psalm 136 Scripture for Memorization/Meditation

O give thanks to the LORD, for He is good,
for His mercy endures forever.
VERSE 1

Verses for Further Memorization/Meditation

- For You, Lord, are good, and ready to forgive, and abundant in mercy to all those who call on You (Psalm 86:5).
- Praise the LORD. O give thanks to the LORD, for He is good, for His mercy endures forever (Psalm 106:1).
- Blessed be the God and Father of our Lord Jesus Christ, who according to His abundant mercy has begotten us again to a living hope through the resurrection of Jesus Christ from the dead (1 Peter 1:3).
- Every good gift and every perfect gift is from above and comes down from the Father of lights, with whom there is no variation or shadow of turning (James 1:17).

Study 28

PSALM 138

Psalm 138 is the first of the final eight recorded psalms of David. In this song, David offers unrestrained praise to God, and for a number of reasons. David gives God credit for the strength in his soul. He had called out to God, and God had answered him, resulting in his praise for God's love and faithfulness.

David's prayer is that *all* earthly kings will hear the words of God and respond with praise, acknowledging His glory. Much will depend on their individual attitudes. God is highly exalted, yet He is always willing to respond to the lowly—those who humble themselves and seek His help. Those who attempt to exalt themselves in pride, however, miss out on God's compassionate help and support.

Psalm 138 Outline

(VERSES 1–3) David's declaration of praise

(VERSES 4–6) Earthly kings shall praise the Lord

(VERSES 7–8) Confidence for the future

A psalm of David.

1I will praise You with my whole heart; before the gods I will sing
praise to You.
2I will worship toward Your holy temple and praise Your
name for Your loving-kindness and for Your truth, for You have
magnified Your word above all Your name.
3In the day when I cried, You answered me and strengthened
me with strength in my soul.
4All the kings of the earth shall praise You, O LORD, when they
hear the words of Your mouth.
5Yes, they shall sing in the ways of the LORD, for great is the
glory of the LORD.
6Though the LORD is high, yet He considers the lowly, but the
proud He knows from afar.
7Though I walk in the midst of trouble, You will revive me.
You shall stretch out Your hand against the wrath of my enemies,
and Your right hand shall save me.
8The LORD will perfect what concerns me. Your mercy, O LORD,
endures forever; do not forsake the works of Your own hands.

Observe

What does David say a believer's response to the Lord should be?

How does God respond to "the lowly" (or humble)?

What does David pray "All the kings of the earth" will do in response to God?

Interpret

What does it mean to give the Lord thanks with your "whole heart"?

....

....

....

....

....

What does the psalmist mean when he says, "before the gods I will sing praise to You"?

....

....

....

....

....

....

Why can believers praise the Lord even in the midst of trouble?

....

....

....

....

....

....

Apply

How can you make praise and worship an important part of your faith?

How have you seen God "revive" you in times of trouble?

In what ways does the written Word of God (the scriptures) inspire you to praise and worship Him?

Psalm 138 Scripture for Memorization/Meditation

Though the LORD is high, yet He considers the lowly, but the proud He knows from afar.
VERSE 6

Verses for Further Memorization/Meditation

- Let everything that has breath praise the LORD. Praise the LORD (Psalm 150:6).
- There are many plans in a man's heart; nevertheless, the counsel of the LORD shall stand (Proverbs 19:21).
- . . .that at the name of Jesus every knee should bow, of things in heaven and things in earth and things under the earth, and that every tongue should confess that Jesus Christ is Lord, to the glory of God the Father (Philippians 2:10–11).
- "For I know the thoughts that I think toward you," says the LORD, "thoughts of peace and not of evil, to give you an expected end. Then you shall call on Me and you shall go and pray to Me, and I will listen to you" (Jeremiah 29:11–12).

Study 29

PSALM 139

Psalm 139 is an amazing expression of God's loving familiarity with David and David's unrelenting devotion in return. His description of God's awareness of his life might be off-putting for many people. God is watching when the psalmist wakes up, goes to bed, sits down, and gets up. He knows every word David says and thinks.

How does David feel about the close scrutiny of God? It depends on how one interprets his comments. When he writes of being beset, both behind and before, and of having the hand of God upon him, does he feel restricted? Protected? Is he describing futile attempts to carve out a little personal time and space for himself? Or is he speculating about the unlimited ability of God to watch over him wherever he might find himself—heights or depths, day or night, one side of the sea or the other? Either way, his musings have shown him that the omnipresence of God is both too lofty and too wonderful for him to absorb.

Psalm 139 Outline

(VERSES 1–6) God knows us. . .intimately

(VERSES 7–12) God is always with us

(VERSES 13–16) Fearfully and wonderfully made

(VERSES 17–18) God's precious thoughts toward us

(VERSES 19–22) A deep desire for righteousness and justice

(VERSES 23–24) A humble prayer

To the chief musician, a psalm of David.

1 O Lord, You have searched me and known me.
2 You know when I sit down and when I rise up; You understand
my thought from afar.
3 You surround my path and my lying down and get acquainted
with all my ways.
4 For there is not a word on my tongue, but behold, O Lord,
You know it altogether.
5 You have surrounded me behind and before and laid Your
hand on me.
6 Such knowledge is too wonderful for me; it is high; I cannot
attain it.
7 Where shall I go from Your Spirit? Or where shall I flee from
Your presence?
8 If I ascend up into heaven, You are there. If I make my bed
in hell, behold, You are there.
9 If I take the wings of the morning and dwell in the uttermost
parts of the sea,
10 even there Your hand shall lead me and Your right hand
shall hold me.
11 If I say, "Surely the darkness shall cover me, even the night
shall be light around me,"
12 yes, the darkness does not hide from You, but the night
shines as the day. The darkness and the light are both alike to You.
13 For You have formed my inmost being. You have woven me
in my mother's womb.
14 I will praise You, for I am fearfully and wonderfully made.
Marvelous are Your works, and my soul knows that very well.
15 My substance was not hidden from You when I was made
in secret and skillfully formed in the lowest parts of the earth.
16 Your eyes saw my substance, yet being imperfect, and in
Your book all my members were written, which in continuance
were fashioned, when as yet there were none of them.
17 How precious also are Your thoughts to me, O God! How
great is the sum of them!
18 If I were to count them, they would be more in number than
the sand. When I awake, I am still with You.

[19]Surely You will slay the wicked, O God. Depart from me
therefore, you murderous men!
[20]For they speak against You wickedly, and Your enemies take
Your name in vain.
[21]Do I not hate those who hate You, O LORD? And am not I
grieved with those who rise up against You?
[22]I hate them with perfect hatred; I count them my enemies.
[23]Search me, O God, and know my heart; test me, and know
my thoughts,
[24]and see if there is any wicked way in me, and lead me in
the way everlasting.

Observe

How did David describe God's knowledge of him?

....

....

....

What does David request of God in this psalm?

....

....

....

What attributes of God are depicted in Psalm 139?

....

....

....

....

Interpret

What does Psalm 139 reveal about God's care for us throughout our lives?

What caused David to offer his praise to God?

Why would David want God to examine his heart?

Apply

How does this psalm motivate you to praise the Lord and thank Him for His goodness in your life?

What gift of praise could you give God today?

How can you remind yourself that His presence is always with you?

Psalm 139 Scripture for Memorization/Meditation

I will praise You, for I am fearfully and wonderfully made.
Marvelous are Your works, and my soul knows that very well.
VERSE 14

Verses for Further Memorization/Meditation

- When I consider Your heavens, the work of Your fingers, the moon and the stars, which You have ordained, what is man that You are mindful of him? And the son of man that You care about him? (Psalm 8:3–4).
- "Therefore go and teach all nations, baptizing them in the name of the Father and of the Son and of the Holy Spirit, teaching them to observe all the things that I have commanded you. And behold, I am with you always, even to the end of the world" (Matthew 28:19–20).
- For we are His workmanship, created in Christ Jesus for good works, which God has before ordained that we should walk in them (Ephesians 2:10).
- He has shown you, O man, what is good. And what does the LORD require of you, but to do justice and to love mercy and to walk humbly with your God? (Micah 6:8).

Study 30

PSALM 143

Psalm 143 (along with 6, 32, 38, 51, 102, and 130) is classified among the "penitential" psalms, the final one of this category in the book. Although similar in content to many of David's other psalms, this one contains his acknowledgment that he is among the unrighteous people worthy of judgment, and he asks to be spared.

David's condition leads him to request God to answer quickly. Those who go down to the pit are people who die. The darkness in David's life is severe. He needs light, so he asks the Lord for relief by the morning. His trust remains in God, and he is eager for God to act.

Psalm 143 Outline

(VERSES 1–2)	Pleading for God's ear
(VERSES 3–4)	David's crisis
(VERSES 5–6)	God's works in the past
(VERSE 7)	David's plea for an answer
(VERSE 8)	The Lord's loving guidance
(VERSE 9)	Deliverance from evil men
(VERSE 10)	Learning God's good will
(VERSES 11–12)	A prayer for revival and rescue

A psalm of David.

1 Hear my prayer, O Lord, give ear to my supplications; in Your
faithfulness answer me, and in Your righteousness.

2 And do not enter into judgment with Your servant, for in
Your sight no man living shall be justified.

3 For the enemy has persecuted my soul; he has struck my life
down to the ground; he has made me to dwell in darkness, like
those who have been long dead.

4 Therefore my spirit is overwhelmed within me; my heart is
desolate within me.

5 I remember the days of old; I meditate on all Your works; I
muse on the work of Your hands.

6 I stretch out my hands to You; my soul thirsts for You, like
a thirsty land. *Selah*.

7 Hear me speedily, O Lord. My spirit fails; do not hide Your
face from me, lest I be like those who go down into the pit.

8 Cause me to hear Your loving-kindness in the morning, for
in You I trust. Cause me to know the way in which I should walk,
for I lift up my soul to You.

9 Deliver me, O Lord, from my enemies. I flee to You to hide me.

10 Teach me to do Your will, for You are my God. Your Spirit
is good; lead me into the land of uprightness.

11 Revive me, O Lord, for Your name's sake; for Your righteousness' sake bring my soul out of trouble.

12 And by Your mercy cut off my enemies and destroy all those
who afflict my soul, for I am Your servant.

Observe

To which of the Lord's character traits does David appeal?

What is the focus of this prayer?

What imagery did David use to communicate his dire need?

Interpret

What can believers learn from how David handled his fears and problems?

What strategies would be best to use as we combat feelings of doubt or discouragement?

How does God teach His people the lessons He wants us to learn?

Apply

What attitude does God want you to have toward yourself?

In what area of your life do you need God's leading most right now?

How does remembering God's past faithfulness encourage you to trust Him with your current struggles?

Psalm 143 Scripture for Memorization/Meditation

Revive me, O LORD, for Your name's sake; for Your righteousness' sake bring my soul out of trouble.
VERSE 11

Verses for Further Memorization/Meditation

- I love the LORD because He has heard my voice and my supplications. Because He has inclined His ear to me, therefore I will call on Him as long as I live (Psalm 116:1–2).
- "Beware, lest you forget the LORD who brought you out of the land of Egypt, from the house of bondage" (Deuteronomy 6:12).
- Will You not revive us again, that Your people may rejoice in You? (Psalm 85:6).
- If any of you lacks wisdom, let him ask of God, who gives to all men generously and without reproach, and it shall be given him (James 1:5).